JADE OF SHIMAO

石峁玉器

神木市石峁文化研究会 编

图书在版编目（ＣＩＰ）数据

石峁玉器 ／ 神木市石峁文化研究会编. —— 北京 ：
文物出版社，2018.5 （2022.2 重印）
ISBN 978-7-5010-5562-3

Ⅰ．①石… Ⅱ．①神… Ⅲ．①龙山文化－古玉器－神
木县－图录 Ⅳ．①K876.82

中国版本图书馆CIP数据核字(2018)第049373号

石峁玉器

编　　者	神木市石峁文化研究会

责任编辑　徐　旸
再版编辑　马晨旭
责任印制　陈　杰

出版发行　文物出版社
社　　址　北京市东城区东直门内北小街 2 号楼
网　　址　http://www.wenwu.com
邮　　箱　web@wenwu.com
制版印刷　北京图文天地制版印刷有限公司
经　　销　新华书店
开　　本　889×1194　1/16
印　　张　24
版　　次　2018年5月第1版
印　　次　2022 年 2 月第 2 次印刷
书　　号　ISBN 978-7-5010-5562-3
定　　价　660.00元

《石峁玉器》编委会

主　　任：胡文高

副 主 任：古　方　刘云辉

顾　　问：李伯谦　李三原

委　　员：康兰英　项世荣　苏永华　李建军

　　　　　王保平　孙世瑾　康元利　黄超远

编　　辑：徐　旸

摄　　影：宋　朝　王保平

器物说明：李红娟

目 录

前　言
神秘的石峁　神奇的古玉

神木市石峁文化研究会

所谓石峁玉器，就是出土于石峁遗址的玉制器物。长期以来，人们习惯地把这类"古玉"统称为石峁玉器。石峁玉器和其他史前玉器一样，同是古玉大家庭的一员。可惜的是，石峁玉器最早现世于民间，大部分沦落市肆、漂泊四海，有的甚至被当地的农民卖进了农副产品收购站[1]。在业界，一直是只闻其名，难觅其影。到了20世纪中后期，随着石峁遗址和石峁玉器相继被发现的消息传开后，石峁才逐步进入了人们的视线，尤其是那数量庞大、造型奇特、制作精美的玉器，更是闻名遐迩、引人关注。遗憾的是，当时的石峁遗址还未进行大规模的考古发掘，可供参考的资料几乎为零，所见玉器的埋藏性质、年代、文化背景以及玉器与遗址之间的关系等主要问题一直没有准确的定论，致使对石峁玉文化的研究一直停留在认识阶段。时至今日，很难找到一部有关石峁玉器的专业论著，为了弥补这一空白，尽快将石峁玉文化的研究纳入我国古玉文化研究的范畴而提供第一手参考资料，神木市石峁文化研究会在上级各业务部门和神木市委、市政府的大力支持下，经古方、刘云辉二位玉器研究专家精心指导并严格把关后，从神木市博物馆和神木市石峁文化研究会珍藏的石峁玉器中，筛选出一批

具有鲜明地域风格和时代特征的石峁玉文化代表器编纂成册，聊表心愿，以飨同道。

一、石峁传奇

提及石峁玉器必先了解石峁。石峁是陕北地区一个偏僻的小山村，位于陕西北部毛乌素沙漠南沿，隶属于神木市高家堡镇。村庄座落在秃尾河北岸与洞川沟交汇处的梁峁上，和牛沙墕、雷家墕、樊庄则等自然村落相邻，地表沟壑纵横，梁峁相连，是典型的黄土丘陵地貌，平均海拔在1100~1300米之间。（图一）

石峁村始于何年，目前无据可查。但神秘的传说由来已久，具有关资料整理记述，主要有：

1. 皇城台的传说

在石峁村西南边，有一座用石头围砌起来的平顶山峁，当地人把这里叫皇城台。相传，这里曾经住过一位"唐朝的公主"。据明朝《延绥镇志》记载，唐太宗贞观三年（公元629年），北方少数民族铁勒有十一个部落归顺唐朝，朝廷在高家堡东五里处的"拔野古都"（今皇城台一带）设置了

幽陵都督府来管理这些部落[2]。清朝道光年间《神木县志》还记载了一段幽陵都督府改设英宁府的传说。唐肃宗乾元元年（公元758年），回纥遣使向唐朝求婚，肃宗便将幼女宁国公主下嫁于磨延啜和亲，并册封磨延啜为英武威远毗伽可汗，宁国公主被尊称为可敦（王后的意思），不久，可汗去世后，宁国公主带着儿子投奔了唐朝。朝廷将幽陵都督府赐予宁国公主，并更名为英宁府[3]。后来还有"宅门墕堡"之说等等。至于何年又叫皇城台已无明确记载。但根据目前对皇城台的考古发掘表明，皇城台是一处"龙山文化晚期的宫殿建筑群遗址"，是石峁古城的核心建筑区。

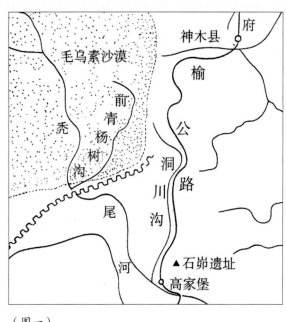

（图一）

2. 三座城的传说

很久以前，石峁周边有"三座城"，分别由姊妹三人带兵把守。有一天调皮的小妹突然在自己把守的城头燃起烽火，正在带兵操练的两个姐姐发现这紧急信号后，火速带兵赶到小妹的守城。当到达城下后并未发现敌情，大姐便生气地质问小妹这是怎么回事？小妹却若无其事地回答说这里并非真有敌情，我只不过是想试探一下你们俩的警惕性。姐俩听后哭笑不得，只好无奈的返回驻地。有一天小妹真的发现了敌情，火速登城点火示警，但两个姐姐总以为又是小妹捣鬼，便没有理睬，造成了三座城先后都被敌人攻占的悲剧[4]。

这个类似狼来了的传说，是当地人根据石峁山上的"三套石城"编造出来的？还是真有其事，暂无可靠依据。

3. 女王坟的传说

距石峁村东边约二公里外，有处地势较高的小山包，南北长约30米，东西宽约50米，地表散落有类似石峁城墙上的石块和少量碎陶片。当地人认为这里就是埋葬"石峁女王"的坟墓，因此得名"女王坟"。

根据《高家堡镇志》记载：上世纪50年代，康家寨子村（女王坟附近的一个村庄）农民康能升，曾经对此坟进行过盗掘，出土的玉器中有玉羊、玉鱼，同时还发现墓葬内有硃砂和陶器。后来调查证实，此处确是一块史前墓地，遗憾的是，大部分已被盗掘破坏。

4. 玉塔村的传说

玉塔村是高家堡镇辖的一个行政村落，地处

永利河边，距离石峁遗址约三公里。传说，这个村河边的台地下埋藏有十八槽、十八瓮珠宝玉器，因此而得名玉塔村[5]。联想到石峁遗址出土有大量玉器，这里地处河边又距离石峁不远，是不是这里就是石峁王国的玉器作坊呢？当然还需要今后考古发掘来证实。

二、发现石城

就是这些传说，一直在支撑着一个事实的存在，那就是神秘的"石峁王国"！

1958年，陕西省为了响应国家号召，在全省范围内开展文物普查工作。同年4月，由省、地、县组成的普查小组来到当时的高家堡人民公社，在公社干部乔世明的带领下，普查人员首次踏上了石峁山。经详细踏勘调查，工作人员发现石峁山上有三套城，并采集到大量的文物标本，根据这些现象，工作人员们分析认为在石峁村与雷家墕村一带，存在一处新石器时代龙山文化遗址。遗址石墙长约2公里，宽约3公里。调查工作结束之后，工作组用"石峁山遗址"命名，向上级有关部门作了书面汇报[6]。但是，这一重大发现，被当时正在轰轰烈烈进行的"大跃进"运动淹没而未被引起重视。

1976年1月，曾供职于原陕西省文物管理委员会干部戴应新，为了抢救在农田基本建设过程中发现的文物，并根据自己掌握的线索，专程来到了神木县（市）高家堡人民公社（镇）石峁大队（村），在大队支部书记牛德勤的大力协助下，

从当地农民手中征集到了一百余件精美玉器和造型奇特的陶器等文物（现藏于陕西省历史博物馆）。同年9月，戴先生再次来到石峁对遗址进行了详细调查。

1977年戴先生在认真研究了所征集玉器等文物的基础上，结合对遗址的调查情况综合分析认为，"石峁遗址是一处规模宏大、遗存丰富的龙山文化遗址"。所征集的玉器等文物属同一时期遗物。随即，戴先生将这些研究成果以及玉器的照片等资料，分别在有关刊物予以公布[7]。从此石峁遗址和石峁玉器才真正得到了考古科学意义上的认可和各级政府的高度重视。

1983年，石峁遗址被公布为"神木县第二批重点文物保护单位"。

1992年4月，石峁遗址被公布为"陕西省重点文物保护单位"。

2006年，国务院又将石峁遗址确立为第六批全国重点文物保护单位。

由于石峁遗址地处荒野，又属黄土丘陵地带，很容易遭受自然和农耕等人为破坏。为了切实有效保护遗址，更进一步地了解遗址的遗存性质等问题，神木市政府曾多次向上级主管部门请示汇报并要求对遗址进行抢救性发掘。2011年，在陕西省文物局的高度重视和大力推动下，由陕西省考古研究院、榆林市文物考古勘探工作队、神木市文体广电局参与的石峁遗址联合考古工作队，再次对遗址开展了区域系统考古调查和重点复查，发现了由皇城台、内城和外城三个层次构成的石城以及城门、墩台、马面、角台等附属建筑，城

内面积达 400 万平方米以上[8]。

2012 年经国家文物局批准，联合考古队重点对外城东门遗址及城内后阳湾、呼家洼、韩家圪旦等地点进行了选择性发掘，揭露了规模宏大、建筑精良的外城东门遗址和成排分布的房址、高等级墓葬等遗迹，出土了一批具有断代意义的陶、玉、石、骨器等遗物[9]，并确认石峁遗址是一处公元前 2300 至公元前 1800 年间中国所见规模最大的城址。其建筑宏伟、结构合理、防御功能完备，堪称"华夏第一城"。

石峁古城的发现，被誉为是本世纪十分重要的考古新发现。2013 年 1 月 13 日，被中国社会科学院评为"中国考古新发现"；2013 年 4 月又高票入选"2012 年度全国十大考古新发现"；2013 年 8 月，在世界考古上海论坛会议上也被评为"2011~2012 年度 10 项世界重大田野考古发现之一"。此后，中央电视台《新闻联播》《新闻频道》《科教频道》及地方媒体多次进行了报道。同时，央视 10 频道以《石破天惊》为题，制作了四集专题片在《探索与发现》栏目进行了播放。央视 4 套也制作了三集专题片，在《国宝档案》栏目对石峁遗址的考古成果进行了详细介绍，获得了社会各界的高度关注[10]。

石峁遗址的发现，不只是让我们认识了一座史前最大石城，更重要的是为我们重新理解公元前 2000 年前后，在华夏大地上"万邦林立"的社会图景，提供了重要的启示意义[11]。同时，也为我们重新认识早期国家的形成与古代文明的内涵提供了有力的支撑。

三、玉出石峁

石峁遗址的现世，离不开石峁玉器的贡献。人们最早认识石峁遗址还是从那无名的石峁玉器开始的。

石峁出土玉器，最早可追溯到清朝晚期，由于当时国情所限基本上都流失于海外。直到 20 世纪 60~70 年代，随着大量古玉的出现，人们追根溯源，才知道这些奇形怪状的玉器原来出自石峁山上。但惋惜的是，这些重要信息不仅并未能引起人们重视，而且当地农副公司还将大量收购的石峁玉器当做"玉料"转卖外贸公司出口换汇了[12]。粗略估计，目前流散于世的石峁玉器少说也有三四千件。如此数量的玉器惨遭流失，对于石峁遗址乃至国家而言无疑是一个不可估量且无法挽回的损失。为了减少损失挽救石峁遗址，神木市石峁文化研究会（简称研究会）在会长胡文高的带动下，有针对性地对石峁玉器以及其他各类文物展开了抢救性征集。截至目前，共征集到玉器约 400 多件、陶器 300 多件、石器 200 多件、骨器及其他文物 100 多件、铜镯、铜齿环 10 余件。这批文物除了捐给神木市博物馆 300 多件外，其余的目前仍收藏于研究会展览馆。

石峁玉器，在我国浩瀚的古玉历史长河中虽说是一条小小的支流，但它却是古玉大家庭中重要的成员之一。对它展开研究，不仅是研究石峁文化的基础和补充，也是研究我国龙山文化晚期至夏代早期这段特殊时期古玉文化的重要环节。为此，研究会经请示神木市委市政府同意，在神木市文体广电局的主持下，于 2011 年 12 月、2012 年 7 月，分别在神木召开了两届"石峁玉器研讨会"。来自包括台湾地区在内的全国 70 多位考古、玉学专家和学术权威机构代表莅临并指导了会议。会议期间，代表们除了参观考察了石峁遗址和发掘出土的玉器等文物外，重点对研究会提供的 300 多件玉器及神木市博物馆藏的部分石峁玉器进行了鉴赏分析，并通过与石峁遗址发掘出土的玉器进行比对研究后，大家一致认为：

① 这两次研讨会是近年来少有的"古玉饕餮盛宴"，十分难得。

② 所鉴玉器未见存疑，年代大致与石峁遗址相同。

③ 数量庞大、玉种繁杂、用料考究、工艺精良，堪称"神奇古玉"。

④ 造型新颖、切割薄妙，独创改制是石峁玉器的特点与风格。

⑤ 光如镜面的打磨、细如发丝的雕刻、繁如锦簇的镂空等工艺是"鬼斧神工"的真实体现。

⑥ 玉璇玑与铜齿环巧妙的结合，给玉璇玑的功用提供了新的信息，全国尚属首例，弥足珍贵。

⑦ 石峁玉器的神奇现世，实属罕见，是中国古玉文化研究领域的一块"处女地"，大有文章可作。

专家们的评价，既是对石峁玉器的概括与总结，也是对我们工作的认可与鼓励。对此我们既感荣幸又觉责任重大，在保护国家文物的道路上，还需坚韧不拔继续前行。

关于石峁玉器的详情，已有古方和刘云辉二位专家在专论中详细描述，这里我们就不再赘述了。十分感谢二位专家的无私奉献与不吝赐教。同时也对长期以来一直关心和支持帮助我们的各级领导、各位专家、学者以及同仁志士表示衷心的感谢，并致以崇高的敬意。

对石峁玉文化的研究，正如专家所言，"是有文章可作"。但苦于我辈才疏学浅，深感心有余而力不足，要做大做好石峁玉器这篇巨文，还需紧紧依靠各级政府和社会各界的大力支持。在此，我们仅以一个"保管员"的身份，用抛砖引玉的形式向大家提供一点参考资料，出现谬误或差错，还请原谅，诚请赐教，我们不胜感激。

孤雁难成行，众志可成城，我们相信在党和国家的英明正确领导下，有各级政府的大力支持，充分利用社会各界的智慧与力量精诚合作，不仅石峁玉文化的文章能够做好、做大，而且石峁遗址历史文化研究的春天也指日可待。

执笔：胡文高

2017 年 9 月 20 日

注释：

[1] 戴应新：《我与石峁龙山文化玉器》，《中国玉学、玉文化论丛》，紫禁城出版社，2004年4月。

[2] 范佩伟：《高家堡史话》，陕西人民出版社，2015年10月。

[3][4][5] 同[2]。

[6]《高家堡镇志》第九篇《文物胜迹》。

[7] 戴应新：《陕西神木县石峁龙山文化遗址调查》，《考古》，1977年第三期。

[8] 孙周勇、邵晶：《发现石峁古城》，《石峁：过去、现在与未来》，文物出版社，2016年8月。

[9][10][11] 同[8]。

[12]同[1]

第一届石峁玉器鉴赏座谈会现场

讨会合影留念

2012.7.20

第二届石峁玉器研讨会合影

PREFACE
MYSTERIOUS SHIMAO, AMAZING ANCIENT JADE

Shimao Culture Research Society

Shimao jade ware is jade items unearthed at Shimao Site. For a long time, people have generally referred to ancient jade ware of this type as Shimao jade ware. Shimao jade ware, like other prehistoric jade ware, is a member of the jade ware family. Unfortunately, it was first discovered by people ignorant of its value; most of it has been traded across the world. Some were even sold by ignorant farmers to farm and sideline product purchasing stations [1]. Thus in archaeological circles, it had been heard of but hard to find. It was not until the mid and late 20th century when the discoveries of Shimao Site and Shimao jade came around that Shimao gradually caught people's attention. The large number of uniquely-designed, exquisitely-crafted jade ware, in particular, enjoyed widespread renown and drew much attention. Regrettably, large-scale archaeological excavations have not been carried out at Shimao Site then. There are very little available reference materials. There have not been definite conclusions on such major questions as nature, date and cultural background of the jade and the relationship between the jade and the site. Consequently, research on Shimao jade culture has stayed in the perceptual stage. So far, it is still hard to find a dissertation on Shimao jade. To fill the gap

and provide first-hand materials for studies on Shimao jade culture, which should be categorized into research on ancient jade culture, Shimao Culture Research Society in Shenmu, with the vigorous support of the superior authorities and Shenmu CPC Municipal Committee and Municipal Government, selects from the Shimao jade collections of Shenmu Municipal Museum and of the society a number of representative Shimao jade ware with distinctive local features and characters of the times, collects them into this book, and presents it to the reader.

To talk about Shimao jade, we must first learn about Shimao. Shimao is a remote small village in northern Shaanxi, situated on the south of Maowusu Desert, under the jurisdiction of Gaojiabu Town, Shenmu City. The village, sitting on the hilltop where the north bank of the Tuwei River meets with the Dongchuan Valley, is neighbor of natural villages such as Niushayan, Leijiayan, and Fanzhuangze. With numerous gullies and hills, the area has a terrain typical of loess hills, with an average altitude ranging between 1,100m and 1,300m. (Fig.1) There is no historical record on the origin of Shimao Village. But there have been some age-old mysterious legends. The following are some of them:

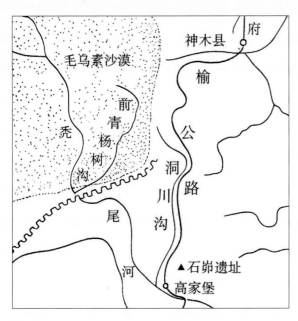

Fig.1

I. Legend of Huangchengtai (royal complex platform)

To the southwest of Shimao Village, there is a flat-topped hill reinforced with stones, known as Huangchengtai, or "Imperial City Terrace", among locals. According to legend, there lived a princess during the Tang Dynasty. As recorded in *Annals of Yansui Town* in the Ming Dynasty, "In the 3rd year of Zhenguan (629 CE) under the reign of Emperor Taizong of Tang, eleven tribes of the Tiele people, an ethnic minority in the north, pledged allegiance to the Tang Dynasty. The court set up Youling Area Command at the "ancient capital of Baye" (now around Huangchengtai) *five li* to the east of Gaojiabao, to administer these tribes [2]. Besides, *History of Shenmu County* written in the years of Daoguang in the Qing Dynasty records a story how Youling Area Command was changed to Yingning

Prefecture. In the first year of Qianyuan(758CE) under the reign of Emperor Suzong of Tang, Uighur sent an envoy to the imperial court of the Tang Dynasty and asked for marriage. Emperor Suzong thus married his young daughter Princess Ningguo to Moyanchuo and conferred him a title Valiant Bilge Khagan with Might Pacifying the Distance. Princess Ningguo was called Kedun ("Queen") respectfully. Before long, after the khan passed away, Princess Ningguo went to the Tang Dynasty with her son. The court made Youling Area Command her fief and renamed it Yingning Prefecture [3]. It is said to have had another name "Zhaimenyan Castle". As for when it was renamed Huangchengtai, there is no clear record. However, archaeological excavation of Huangchengtai has shown that Huangchengtai is a site of palace complex architecture in the late period of Longshan Culture and sits in the core area of Shimao Ancient City.

II. Legend of Three Cities

Long, long ago, there were three cities in the neighborhood of Shimao, guarded respectively by three sisters. One day, the youngest sister, a naughty girl, lit the beacon at the castle she defended. Her two sisters, who were drilling troops, rushed to rescue her castle at the signal of emergency. When they arrived and found no sign of enemy, the eldest sister reprimanded her and asked her what that was all about. The reckless girl replied nonchalantly that there was no enemy attack and she was just testing if her two elder sisters were vigilant enough. Her sisters thus had no choice but to return to their respective castles. One day, the youngest sister really found an enemy assault. She hurried to light the beacon. But her sisters thought she was doing mischief again and ignored the alarm. As a result, the three castles were captured by their enemy one by one. [4]

It cannot be verified so far whether this legend, similar to the story "Shepherd Boy and Wolves", was made up by locals based on the "three castles" on Shimao Mountain or was a true happening.

III. Legend of the Queen's Tomb

About two kilometers to the east of Shimao Village, there is a rather high mound, stretching about 30 meters from south to north and about 50 meters from east to west. Scattered on the ground there are stone blocks which seem to have been used for city walls, as well as a few number of broken pottery pieces. Local people believe that this is the tomb where the Queen of Shimao was buried, hence the name Nüwangfen, or "the Queen's Tomb".

As recorded in *Annals of Gaojiapu Town*, in the 1950s, Kang Nengsheng, a farmer from KangjiaZhaizi Village (a village near the Queen's Tomb), robbed the tomb and discovered some jade ware including jade sheep and jade fish, and some cinnabar and pottery ware. It was later confirmed that this is indeed a prehistoric tomb. Unfortunately, it has been destroyed by robbery.

IV. Legend of Yuta Village

Yuta Village is an administrative village under the jurisdiction of Gaojiabao Town, by the Yongli River, about three kilometers to Shimao Site. Legend has it that eighteen trenches of jade and eighteen jars of jade are buried somewhere near the village. Hence the name Yuta (lit."Jade Pagoda") Village. Considering that a large amount of jade ware has been unearthed at Shimao Site and the village located by the river is not far from Shimao, is the

village the site of the jade workshop of Shimao Kingdom? Of course, this needs to be verified through archaeological excavations in the future.

Discovery of the Old City

The legends have testified to the existence of the mysterious kingdom of Shimao!

In 1958, to respond to the call of the state, the government of Shaanxi Province carried out the first province-wide cultural heritage survey. In April of the same year, a survey team consisting of personnel from the relevant departments of the province, prefecture and county arrived at Gaojiabao People's Commune. Guided by Qiao Shiming, an official of the commune, the survey team set foot on Shimao Mountain for the first time. After detailed surveying and investigation, archaeologists discovered that there were "three cities" (Huangchengtai, inner city and outer city) at the place and collected large quantities of cultural specimen specimens. Based on these findings, archaeologists believed that there was a Neolithic site of Longshan Culture around Shimao Village and Leijiayan Village. The stone wall system of the site was about 2 kilometers long and around 3 kilometers wide. After the investigation was over, the work team named the site Shimao Mountain Site and submitted a written report [6] to the authorities concerned. However, this major discovery was neglected in the boisterous "Great Leap Forward" Movement.

In January 1976, Dai Yingxin, an official of Shaanxi Administrative Commission of Cultural Heritage, made a special trip to Shimao Production Brigade (Village), Gaojiabao People's Commune (Town), Shenmu County (City), based on the clues he grasped, in order to rescue the cultural relics discovered in the course of farmland infrastructure construction. With the assistance of Niu Deqin, CPC branch secretary of the Production Brigade, Dai collected over 100 exquisite jades and uniquely-shaped pottery ware (now collected in Shaanxi History Museum). In September of the same year, he paid a second visit to Shimao and made a detailed investigation on the site.

In 1977, after carefully investigating the cultural relics including the jade ware and comprehensively analyzing the circumstances of the site, Dai concluded that "Shimao Site is a large-scale site of Longshan Culture with abundant cultural heritage", and the cultural relics collected, including the jade ware, could date back to the same period. Then, he published his research results and the photos of the jade ware in relevant journals [7]. It was not until then that Shimao Site and Shimao jade ware truly won archaeological recognition and great attention from governments at different levels.

In 1983, Shimao Site was publicly inscribed by Shenmu County on its Second List of Key Historic Site under Protection.

In April 1992, Shimao Site was declared a key historic site under protection of Shaanxi Province.

In 2006, the State Council inscribed Shimao Site on the 6th List of Key Historic Site under State Protection.

Because Shimao Site is located in the wilderness of loess hills, it is susceptible to damage by nature and human activities such as farming. To protect the site effectively and gain a better understanding of the nature of the site, Shenmu Municipal Government made a report to the superior competent department for many times, asking to carry out rescue excavations of the site. In 2011, with the vigorous support of Shaanxi Provincial Administration of Cultural Heritage, a joint archaeological team was formed by Shaanxi Provincial Institute of Archaeology, Yulin Cultural Heritage Exploration Work Team and Shenmu County Cultural Artifact Bureau to launch the first regional comprehensive investigation and focused review of Shimao Site. They discovered the stone city consisting of Huangchengtai, the inner and outer cities and their auxiliary constructions such as city gates, piers and corner terraces, with a total area of over four million square meters within the city [8].

In 2012, with the approval of the State Administration of Cultural Heritage, a joint archaeological team carried out selective excavation of the east gate to the outer city and spots inside the city such as Houyangwan, Hujiawa and HanjiaGedan, uncovering the site of the well-built large-scale east gate to the outer city and the remains of rows of houses and high-class tombs, unearthing a large number of relics that can serve as dating references, including pottery, jade, stone and bone ware. The team concluded definitely that Shimao Site was the largest site of a city during 2300-1800 BCE discovered so far. It can be said to be First City in China because of its magnificent architecture, good structure and full-fledged defense facilities.

Shimao Ancient Town is reputed as the most important archaeological discovery in the 21st century. On January 13, 2013, it was named New Archaeological Discovery in China; in April 2013, it was elected into the Top Ten New Archaeological Discoveries of China in 2012; in August 2013, it was included in the 10 World Major Field Archaeological Discoveries of 2011-2012 at the Shanghai Archaeology Forum. Later, multiple channels of CCTV and local media covered the discovery many times. CCTV-10 also made a four-episode feature titled *Groundbreaking Discovery* (*Shi-po Tian-jing*) and played it in the program Exploration and Discovery. CCTV-4 also made a three-episode feature, which gives a detailed introduction to the archaeological findings at Shimao Site via the program Archives of State Treasures. The site has thus won much attention from all walks of life.

The discovery of Shimao Site enables us not only to know the greatest prehistoric stone city, but more importantly to shed light on, and update our understanding of, the social landscape in which numerous states coexisted in China around 2000 BCE[11]. Meanwhile, it also provides strong support for us to form a new understanding of the making of early states and ancient civilization.

Jade of Shimao

Shimao Site would not come to light without its jade ware. People first got to know Shimao Site because of the then unknown jade ware.

The unearthing of jade ware at Shimao can be traced back to the late Qing Dynasty. Nearly all the earliest unearthed jade ware at Shimao have drifted overseas due to the national situation then. It was not until the 1960s-70s when large quantities of ancient jade were discovered that people came to know that these strange-looking jade articles came from Shimao Mountain. However, unfortunately, the important information failed to capture people's attention. Local purchasing stations of agricultural and sideline products bought Shimao jade ware in bulk and sold it to foreign trade companies as jade materials for foreign currencies[12]. It is estimated that at least 3,000-4,000 pieces of Shimao jade ware have

been lost in this way—an inestimable, irrecoverable loss for Shimao Site and the state. To reduce the losses and rescue Shimao Site, Shenmu Shimao Culture Research Society (referred to the Society hereinafter), led by Hu Wengao, its president, has launched a rescue collection of Shimao jade and other types of cultural relics. Up to now, over 400 jade articles, over 300 pottery articles, over 200 stone items, over 100 bone & other articles, and more than 10 bronze bracelets and tooth rings have been collected. Besides the over 300 which have been donated to Shenmu Museum, the rest are still on display at the exhibition hall of the Society.

Shimao jade ware is merely a small part of the long history of China's ancient jade, but it is one of the important members of the family of ancient jade. Research on Shimao jade ware lays the foundation for, and constitutes a supplement to, studies on Shimao culture; moreover, it is an important link in research on ancient jade culture from the late period of Longshan Culture to the early stage of the Xia Dynasty in China. Therefore, with the consent of Shenmu CPC Municipal Committee and Municipal Government, Shenmu County Cultural Artifact Bureau sponsored two symposiums on Shimao jade ware respectively in December 2011 and July 2012. More than seventy archaeologists, jade experts and representatives from academic organizations attended the symposiums. During the meetings, besides visiting Shimao site and appreciating the cultural relics unearthed, including the jade ware, the attendees mainly studied the over 300 jade items provided by the society and some Shimao jade ware in the collection of Shenmu Museum. After a comparison with the jade ware unearthed at the site, they reached the following consensuses:

1. The two symposiums were "feasts of ancient jade" that were seldom seen in recent years;

2. The jades studied raise no doubt and date roughly to the same period as the Shimao Site.

3. Marked by large quantities, great variety, quality materials and superb processing techniques, the jade ware can be said to be "wonderful and remarkable";

4. Novel shape, fine and ingenious cutting and original recreation are the features that constitute the style of Shimao jade ware;

5. Smooth polishing, hair-thin carving and elaborate hollowed-out work are evidence of the superb craftsmanship;

6. The ingenious combination of the jade *xuan-ji* and bronze toothed ring shed light on the function of the jade *xuan-ji*—as the first combination of this type, it is especially valuable;

7. Shimao jade ware is indeed very rare and, as a virgin land of Chinese ancient ware research, it calls for much research.

The judgments made by the experts are not only summarizations and summaries of Shimao jade ware, but also praises and encouragements of our work, for this we feel honored and need to take heavy responsibilities. On the road of state cultural heritage protection, we should continue to press ahead with determination.

Gu Fang and Liu Yunhui, the two experts, have provided a detailed description of Shimao stone ware, saving us the trouble of doing it again here. Our thanks go to the two experts for their selfless contribution and enlightening guidance. We'd also like to extend our heartfelt thanks and high regard to leaders at different levels, experts, scholars and colleagues for their concern and support.

Research on Shimao jade culture, as some experts put it, "has a lot of work to do". However, despite our motivation, we have felt our lack of capability to do a thorough research on Shimao jade ware. The vigorous support of governments at all levels and all walks of life is still needed. Therefore, as the "keeper" of the cultural heritage, we cannot but provide some reference materials which we hope may inspire others. If some materials herein are found identical with others elsewhere, it is merely a coincidence and cannot be considered as plagiarism. Should there be any error or mistake, please forgive us and kindly let us know. We will be grateful for that.

A single soldier cannot form an array, and a common will gets a job done. We believe that under the leadership of the Party and the central government, with the vigorous support of governments at all levels, making full use of the wisdom and strengths of all walks of life, we can do well in research on Shimao jade culture. The spring of studies on Shimao Site is around the corner.

Written by Hu Wengao
September 20, 2017

専論一
超级石城 神奇玉器

刘云辉

石峁遗址位于陕西省神木市高家堡镇，这里属黄土高原北部、毛乌素大沙漠的南缘，黄河支流秃尾河及洞川沟交汇的台塬梁峁上。对石峁遗址的认识曾经历了一个漫长的过程。

1958年，陕西省开展文物普查工作，将其命名为"石峁山遗址"[1]。

1963年，陕西省考古工作者和西北大学老师曾在此调查，并记录"石峁山遗址"，断其为石峁文化遗存，面积约10万平方米[2]。

1975年冬季，陕西省文管会戴应新先生到神木县高家堡镇开展文物调查，该镇收购站老收购员段海田告诉戴说，附近石峁地方老出玉器，都是当地村民在生产活动中发现的卖给收购站，县外贸每年下来收购两次，每次都能买到十多件到数十件不等的玉器。从他来收购站十年从未中断过，总计至少收到一千五六百件。县外贸将玉器转售北京总公司，加工出口，赚取外汇。当时只择其质地莹润、厚大精致者收购，凡质差粗黑或薄小者一律不收，估计还有不少玉器散落在各家各户中。戴应新得知这一情况后，表示他现在愿意以较高的价钱收购还在村民手中的玉器，先后四次共收购了石峁玉器126件。

为了弄清楚这些玉器出土情况，戴应新还清理了一座位于石峁小学路旁的石椁墓，在墓主人胸部有一件扇形玉璜，未发现大件玉器[3]。

1981年，中国社会科学院考古研究所张长寿先生在石峁遗址调查，见到了石峁村民收藏的玉牙璋、玉刀、玉璧、玉璜、玉斧、玉钺等，他征集了其中3件[4]。

西安半坡博物馆也于1981年对石峁遗址进行了小面积试掘，发现了石棺葬和瓮棺葬等，采集到包含玉器、石器、骨器、陶器等物[5]。

1986年，陕西省考古研究所吕智荣先生对石峁遗址进行了调查[6]。

在吕智荣调查之后的若干年，榆林市文物管理部门和神木县文体局等单位先后多次对该遗址进行调查，并征集到一些包括玉器在内的遗物[7]。

2010年，神木县人民政府报请陕西省文物局，请求派遣具有考古资质的专业单位对石峁遗址进行抢救性发掘，笔者当时在省文物局分管考古工作，在神木县的文件上签发了"请陕西省考古研究院尽快安排考古发掘，并向国家文物局报送发掘申请，所需经费先由神木县解决"的意见。

2011年，由陕西省考古研究院、榆林市文物考古勘探队、神木县文体广电局组成的联合调查队，对石峁遗址进行了大面积调查。这次调查发现石峁遗址比以往的调查范围更广，工作更为细致，其技术手段和方法更为先进，调查的结果完全超出人们的想象。

2012年，经国家文物局批准，由陕西省考古院和市、县文物部门联合组成的考古队，对石峁遗址开始发掘，经过几年的科学调查和考古发掘研究，取得了令学术界极为震惊的丰硕成果，大量证据表明，石峁遗址是一座规模恢宏、布局严整、功能完备、内涵极为丰富，令人叹为观止的中国北方早期文明的超级城址[8]。

一、超级城址

（1）依据 ^{14}C 系列测年和考古学证据证实，石峁城址的始建年代约为公元前 2300 年左右，而废弃年代大约在公元前 1800 年左右，该城使用约 500 年。其面积达 400 余万平方米，是迄今为止所知国内规模最大的龙山晚期至夏代早期阶段的城址[9]。良渚文化有 290 万平方米的古城；陶寺文化中期修建的大城面积已达 280 万平方米；石家河文化的石家河古城约 120 万平方米；根据最新的调查勘探，如果加上石峁古城之外与其有直接关系的遗存范围计算在内，石峁遗址的面积至少在 1000 万平方米。因此仅从规模观察称其为超级城址，毫无夸张之处。

（2）石峁城址由"皇城台"、内城、外城三大部分构成，内外城以石城垣为界，内外城墙长度为 10 千米，宽度约 2.5 米，目前地面所见残高 1 米左右。内城将"皇城台"拱围其中，城墙大致呈东北—西南分布，面积约 210 万平方米；外城是利用内城东南部墙体向东南方向再行扩筑的弧形石墙形成的封闭空间，城内面积约 190 万平方米。"皇城台"为大型宫殿和高级建筑基址的核心分布区，面积不小于 2000 平方米，其北侧为池苑，现存面积约 300 平方米，深约 2 米。最令人震惊的是"皇城台"周边有以多达十级的堑山砌筑的护坡石墙包裹，每层高 3 米左右，局部石墙石条上还雕刻有菱形眼纹。"皇城台"呈底大顶小的金字塔结构，错落有致，坚固雄厚。在"皇城台"周边发现了石雕人头像、鳄鱼骨板、彩绘壁画等。近年考古队对石峁"皇城台"门址进行了发掘，它亦由广场、外瓮城、南北墩台和内瓮城等四部分构成。有石砌的台基道路和护墙，广场在门址最外，面积达 2100 平方米。证据表明，"皇城台"它代表了一个早期王权国家享受族群最高等级规格，它对早期中国都城史和文明史的研究提供了最令人信服的实证。

石峁外城东门址位于外城东北部，门道为东北向，由内外两重瓮城、门道、砌石夯土墩台、门塾、马面等设施组成。这些布局和结构，完全颠覆了人们对中国古城城市建造历史的传统认识。在晚期石墙的根底部的地面上发现了成层成片分布的壁画残块 300 余片。其壁画以白灰面为底，以红、黄、黑、橙等颜色绘出几何图案。北京大学吕宇斐研究员经过观测，认为石峁东城门的方向略偏东北，夏至日太阳升起时，门道内无任何阴影。石峁东城门的设计，反映了石峁居民具有相当发达的天文学知识。

总之，石峁遗址外城东门址是迄今为止所见时代最早、保存完好、体量巨大、结构复杂、筑造技术先进、装饰华丽的城门遗迹，虽经四千余年的风雨剥蚀，现今仍然气势恢宏、高大威严，位于石峁城的制高点，是控制交通，外防内守的坚固屏障，被称之"华夏第一门"名至实归。

（3）大型墓葬，对石峁遗址发掘的墓葬有瓮棺葬、石棺葬及竖穴土坑墓三类，瓮棺葬均为早夭孩童的葬式，与仰韶文化中的瓮棺葬极其相似；石棺葬多为青年人的葬式，它的出现与当地具有丰富的石材有关；竖穴土坑墓最为常见数量最多，皆为成人葬式，其规模和随葬品的差异巨大。在石峁韩家圪旦已发掘的墓葬规模多在 2 平方米以上，最大的一座墓 M1，长约 4 米、宽 3 米、深 6 米，墓室面积达 12 平方米，出土玉器 20 余件，彩绘陶器 10 多件，还有一件金玉合璧的牙轮形器[10]。

（4）杀戮祭祀坑，在外城东门址一带其发现埋藏人头骨遗迹 6 处，每处人头骨数量不等，少则 1 颗，多则 24 颗，对 K1 内的头骨初步鉴定表明，这些被杀戮并深埋早期地基之下的死者以年轻女性居多，这一现象可能与城址修建过程中实施的奠基或祭祀活动有关[11]。

调查表明，巨型的石峁石城亦不是孤立的存在，大约在公元前 2300 年以来，在内蒙古中南部、陕西北部、在晋西北地区大量出现面积从数百乃至数千平方米的聚落。仅陕北的石峁文化石城聚落的数量就有近百处，石峁遗址所处的秃尾河流域的石城聚落就有十几处，正如石峁考古工作者所言，这些聚落对石峁聚落而言就是众星拱月，它们是石峁王权国家的第二或第三级中心，它奠定了石峁王国生存四五百年的强大的社会基础。

石峁遗址以其规模宏大的超级石城，功能齐全的城市布局（宫殿区、高级建筑区、祭坛、人头骨祭祀坑、手工业作坊区、居住区、贵族墓葬区），以及制作大量石雕人头像、制作铜器，尤其制作大量精致的各种玉器等，都反映了石峁古国曾有大量的人口聚居，具有不同层级的社会组织架构，强大而有序的管理职能，能动员调动庞大的社会力量。正如易华先生所言实现了由玉帛古国到玉戈王国的华丽转身，毫无疑问进入夏时期的石峁古国已经跨入了文明时代的门槛。

简言之，近几年对石峁古城的考古调查和勘探以及考古发掘工作，取得了举世瞩目的成果，为学术界进一步研究黄土高原上的早期中国提供了全新的认知。

二、神奇玉器

说石峁玉器的神奇应当包括以下几个方面：

其一，在未进行考古发掘之前，这里发现的玉器都是当地村民在生产劳动中捡到的，或在一些不知用途的坑中挖到的，还有村民说石峁石墙缝中有玉器，这些都是当地群众的说法，由于不是考古发掘品，一些学者对群众的说法半信半疑，也有一些极为谨慎的专家对其时代甚至一些器物的真伪都有存疑，因此，在1996年出版的《中国玉器全集》中未收录任何一件石峁玉器，据了解，编委会曾讨论过是否收录问题，由于怕引起不必要的争议，最后还是决定不收录[12]。近年来在石峁东城门一带的石墙和皇城台墙体中均发现了玉器，这些玉器或发现于墙体倒塌堆积之内，或发现于石块砌筑的墙体外缘，根据出土状况分析，这些玉牙璋、玉铲、玉璜、玉钺等物应是修建过程中有意嵌入墙体内的（陕西省考古院孙周勇院长表示近来在皇城台遗址又发现了玉璇玑）通过考古发掘还证实除了墙体中藏玉之外，在已发掘的大墓中也发现了玉器，在东城墙之外的祭坛（或为是瞭望建筑）也发现了玉器。这就解开了石峁玉器出土地点的谜团[13]。在城墙和宫墙体中插入玉器，此种现象非常独特，说明了石峁统治集团信奉玉是神物的观念，墙中有玉可以增强墙体的神秘力量，玉器这样的神物是抵御外敌入侵的强大精神屏障。

其二，石峁遗址发现的玉器种类庞杂，有玉璧、玉璇玑（牙璧）、玉环、玉牙璋、玉大刀、玉钺、玉琮、玉璜、玉雕人头像、玉笄、玉鸟等等，尤其是发现了时代最早的玉戈。

其三，石峁遗址出土的最具特色的玉器是大型牙璋、大刀、玉璇玑。

石峁遗址出土的牙璋数量至少在百件以上，除了戴应新先生当年征集的28件（还有3件改制的牙璋），绝大多数从石峁出土的牙璋都收藏在美、欧、日等国博物馆；国内以上海博物馆收藏

的石峁牙璋最多[14]。据现有资料可知，石峁牙璋最长的一件为53.5厘米，是1929年由萨尔莫尼收购，藏于德国科伦远东美术馆[15]。近年来，在石峁遗址发掘出土的牙璋至少已有4个不同的个体，尽管已成残器，但其学术价值无疑很高，其玉色、玉质及形制特征综合观察，均证实流失海内外大量的牙璋绝大多数，就是石峁遗址出土的，勿庸置疑。

石峁遗址出土的玉大刀数量亦很多，除了陕西历史博物馆之外，收藏石峁玉大刀较多的是北京故宫博物院，收录在《故宫博物院藏品大系·玉器编》中就有9件，编者将其中8件定为陕西石峁文化，另一件定为石峁文化。笔者认为从玉材、沁色、历史痕迹、形制、工艺特征综合观察，毫无疑问，它们均属神木石峁遗址的器物。而其中的一件5孔玉大刀长达78.7厘米，宽12.8厘米，厚度0.3厘米[16]；石峁遗址出土的另一件较长玉大刀，是戴应新先生征集的一件（此器早年断裂，被登记为两件，陕西历史博物馆保管部工作人员无意中发现它们玉色、厚度一致，两件断茬可以无缝对接，由此证实原为一件，通长71厘米，大端宽11.5厘米，厚度0.25厘米，刀背钻有4孔，在大端一侧雕琢扉棱，其轮廓近似玉神人的侧面形象[17]。

在石峁遗址发现玉器中的璇玑数量也较多，据不完全统计，其数量至少亦在百件以上，而且型制多样，绝大多数选用优质玉材，制作考究。

石峁玉器从工艺特征观察，是器大而薄，尤

其是牙璋，有些厚度甚至不到两毫米，身薄如纸，有几件牙璋其重量仅为三十至五十多克，拿在手中似乎有断裂的危险。四千年前的石峁玉工制作如此大而薄的器物，其工艺之精湛，可视作鬼斧神工。

其四，在石峁遗址出土的众多玉器中，除了石峁玉工自己制作的玉器之外，还有良渚文化的玉琮（改制器），又有石家河文化的玉虎头，鹰形笄，以及齐家文化的玉璧、玉琮等。反映了石峁国势的强盛，或者说石峁古国统治者能够包容开放，广泛吸纳其他文化，为己所用。

其五，石峁遗址出土玉器究竟是在哪里制作的？勿庸讳言，那些良渚文化玉器、石家河文化玉器、齐家文化玉器显然不是在石峁制作的。但那些精致的玉牙璋、玉大刀、玉璇玑等具有代表性的玉器是由石峁玉工在当地制作的。但也有学者甚至认为石峁遗址出土的玉牙璋都是从石家河文化居民中掠夺的[18]。此种观点缺乏足够的证据，是一种对石峁玉器的误读。

其六，从石峁遗址出土的众多玉器来观察，其材质多样，有少量白玉，亦有青白玉，青黄玉，而最具特色玉牙璋和玉大刀绝大多数是用一种较为特殊的黑色墨玉制成的，邓淑苹研究员认为这种玉具有明显的变质作用之前的母岩沉积岩纹理，如不规则团块或波浪条斑，闻广教授曾对这种闪石玉做过取样分析，确知都是由很小的雏晶紧密堆积而成，因而解释了何以可以剖制成大而薄的片状带刃玉器却不会崩碎。邓淑苹研究员还引用陈东和对法国吉美博物馆中的石峁玉器以科技手段检测发现铁离子和锰与镍的含量较高的成果，并提出了可能因为陕北发现了铁、锰含量高的深色闪石玉，制作牙璋和多孔长刀特别薄锐坚韧的观点[19]。

三、神木石峁文化研究会的玉器藏品

石峁玉器的流失至少始自清末，民国时期也曾有大量流失，海外许多博物馆都收藏有石峁玉器，二十世纪六、七十年代当玉材卖，造成了很大的损失，戴应新先生当年的征集功不可没。近十几年的流失情况也很严重。一方面有群众的无意发现，也有个别人利欲熏心，钻了监管缺失的空子，暗中从事违法盗挖活动。胡文高先生为神木市人，出于对家乡文化的挚爱，上世纪九十代以来，因职业关系，耳闻目睹石峁附近的村民家里有玉器、陶器、石器等古物，且有不少已相继流失到了北京、上海、山西、河南等地的藏家手中，他感到十分痛惜，便萌生了征集收购这里发现的古物的念头，由他发起并申请成立了神木市石峁文化研究会，二十余年来投巨资将流失在外地藏家手中的玉器再买回来。其征集出自石峁遗址的陶器、石器、玉器等古物，达上千件之多，其中玉器达数百件。神木石峁文化研究会自成立起就秉持一个基本原则，征集的器物绝不参予倒卖牟利。目的只有一个，就是要将神木市文化的根留在神木，将这些藏品提供给学术界研究，近十几年来到该会来观摩研究的中外学者和社会各界人士达数千人之多。该会还广邀海内外研究中国古代玉器的近百位知名学者，围绕这些流散征集品召开了若干次学术研讨会。

二十世纪八、九十年代以来石峁玉器的流失，究其原因，一是长期以来对它的重要性认识不足，当地群众就仅知道这个地方偶然出玉器，玉器还能卖点小钱，至于什么时代的，有什么用途就更不知道了。二是，众所周知，石峁遗址地处偏僻，面积巨大，上山道路崎曲，远离村庄，人烟稀少，长期以来亦无专门的遗址保管机构，也无指定的文保员看管，从客观上讲保护的难度很大。神木有极丰富的优质煤炭资源，改革开放以来，投资采煤而致富的人数不胜数，而关注并投资抢救征集文物者少之又少。神木市石峁文化研究会经过多年的不懈努力，四处奔波，出钱出力，才使这里发现的玉器绝大部分留在了神木，为研究石峁遗址提供了弥足珍贵的资料。否则，这些重要器物流失，我们将永远很难看到石峁玉器的庐山真面目。正是从这个意义上讲，胡文高先生及神木市石峁文化研究会的收藏功不可没，其贡献是值得肯定的。

神木市石峁文化研究会的玉器藏品，除了尚未有典型完整的牙璋之外，其他种类较为齐全，如大量的玉璧中除常见的，还有有领玉璧、玉璇玑（牙璧）、三联式璇玑、有领式璇玑；玉琮分为高体玉琮和矮体玉琮，以素面为主，亦有分阶式玉琮，也有良渚式玉琮被切割改制的器物；玉璜以弧形窄体璜为多，也有扇形璜；玉钺和玉刀也

有不少，还有柄形器等；还有多种动物形佩玉，如玉蚕、玉鱼，玉蛙、玉蛇、各式玉鸟，虽然并非完全写实，但能够抓住轮廓特点，活灵活现，如在一件片状玉上表现两只背靠背的立鸟（第334页），采用突出外轮廓并加镂空技法，看似简单，但仍栩栩如生；另一件玉鸟佩（第331页），顶部为一回首鸟，下为多只鸟互相联在一起，其上有十字形和互相对称的"£"形镂空，其高超的艺术表现力，充满了灵动。最引人注目的是玉牙璧数量多，形制丰富，工艺精湛。部分玉璧薄如纸，抛磨光洁度之高，令人不可思议。其中一件玉镯形器（第300页），外表阴刻极为纤细的纹样，不用侧光则很难看清，但其纹样仍然是良渚式的，而玉质则特别温润，从玉色和玉质表象观察似乎与良渚有别，这似乎可做两种诠释，要么是石峁玉工自己仿良渚纹样所雕琢，要么是良渚玉工所刻，由石峁玉工加以改制而成。笔者赞成后一种说法，尽管我们在石峁的牙璋和玉刀上都发现了极为纤细的纹样，但这些纹样均是直线或交叉斜线，迄今并未发现良渚式的曲线，玉色和玉质表象不同，笔者以为相同的玉器埋在太湖流域的南方土壤中和埋在陕北黄土高原的土壤中，经历了四千余年之久，其表象必然会不同。

概言之，神木市石峁文化研究会的石峁玉器，种类丰富，绝大多数玉质温润细腻，制作工艺精湛，对于人们认识研究石峁玉器，是弥足珍贵不可多得的文物瑰宝。

今天的石峁遗址，已被国务院公布为全国重点

文物保护单位，当地政府和各级文管部门对该遗址的重要性有了新的认识，当地政府成立了文物保护机构，陕西省人民代表大会常务委员会还专门制定并颁布了《石峁遗址保护条例》，当地干部和群众遵法守法、保护文物的意识有了很大的提高，石峁遗址历史上文物流失的现象不会再重演了。随着考古发掘工作的持续开展，已有多种迹象表明，位于黄土高原上四千年前的石峁古国，还会有更多的令人震惊的秘密面世。

注解：

[1] 范佩伟：《高家堡史话》，陕西人民出版社，2015 年；神木县档案局 1958 年档案资料。

[2] 孙周勇、邵晶：《石峁：过去、现在与未来》，《发现石峁古城》，文物出版社，2016 年。当年对石峁遗址调查后形成的《遗址登记表》，由安志敏转交给巩启明先生保管。

[3] 戴应新：《回忆石峁遗址的发掘与石峁玉器》，《收藏界》2014 年第 5、6 期

[4] 张长寿：《论神木石峁出土的刀形端刃器》，《南中国及邻近地区古文化研究》，香港中文大学出版社，1994 年。

[5] 西安半坡博物馆：《陕西神木石峁遗址调查试掘简报》，《史前研究》，1983 年第 2 期；魏世刚：《陕西神木石峁遗址发掘二三事》，《史前研究 2000》，三秦出版社，2000 年。

[6] 吕智荣：《陕西神木县石峁遗址发现细石器》，《文博》1989 年第 2 期。

[7] 孙周勇、邵晶《石峁：过去、现在与未来》，《发现石峁古城》，文物出版社，2016 年。

[8] 陕西省考古研究院、榆林市文物考古勘探队、神木县文体局：《陕西神木县石峁遗址》，《考古》1983 年第 7 期。

[9] 同 [8]

[10] 邵晶：《石峁遗址》，《陕西省考古研究院年报》，2014 年。

[11] 同 [8]

[12] 杨伯达主编：《中国玉器全集》，河北人民美术出版社，1996 年。

[13] 孙周勇、邵晶：《关于石峁玉器出土背景的几个问题》，《玉魂国魄—中国古代玉器与传统文化学术讨论会文集（六）》，浙江古籍出版社，2011 年。

[14] 林巳奈夫：《中国古玉研究》，台湾艺术图书公司，1997 年。

[15] 2016 年底在郑州召开的《东亚牙璋》学术讨论会上，张尉研究员介绍了上海博物馆收藏

的 12 件石峁牙璋。

[16] 故宫博物院编：《故宫博物院藏品大系·玉器编·1 新石器时代》，紫禁城出版社，安徽美术出版社，2011 年。

[17] 这件器物原编为两个号，即 SSY83、SSY117。

[18] 持石峁牙璋为掠夺观点的是台湾正中大学郭静云教授，其观点见于《牙璋起源刍议—兼谈陕北玉器之谜》，《三峡大学学报》（人文社会科学版）2014 年 9 月第 36 卷第 5 期。

[19] 邓淑苹：《杨家埠、晋侯墓、芦山峁出土四件玉琮再思考》，《玉润东方—大汶口石峁·良渚玉器文化展》，文物出版社，2014 年。

Essay I

A "SUPER" NEOLITHIC CITY AND ITS AMAZING JADE ARTICLES

Liu Yunhui

The Shimao site is located in the present-day town of Gaojiabao, Shenmu County, Shaanxi Province. The area is characterized by loess tablelands, ridges, and mounds where the Tuwei River (a branch of the Yellow River) and the Dongchuan Ravine intersect on the northern section of the Loess (Huangtu) Plateau and at the southernmost end of the Maowusu Desert. People once spent a lengthy period of time becoming familiar with the history of the Shimao site.

In 1958, Shaanxi Province began carrying out a survey of cultural artifacts there, naming the region the "Shimao Mountain site" [1].

In 1963, archaeologists in Shaanxi worked with professors from Northwest University on another survey, recording their findings and assessing the articles there to be the remains of the Shimao culture. The area of the site was estimated at about 100,000 square meters [2].

During the winter of 1975, Dai Yingxin of the Shaanxi Bureau of Cultural Relics began another survey of Gaojiabao. An elderly purchaser, Duan Haitian, from the local purchasing station told Dai that jade articles had been found at the nearby Shimao site by locals while engaged their day-to-day work. After finding such articles, they would sell them to the purchasing station. Twice

a year, people from other regions would come buy the articles, and each time they bought at least a dozen (and upwards of dozens). During his ten years at the station, there had never been a break in such trade, and in total, he had dealt with 1,500 – 1,600 pieces. These traders would then sell the pieces to their headquarters in Beijing where they would be processed and exported. At the time, buyers only wanted pieces that were bright, smooth, large, and refined; pieces that were of lesser quality or those that were thin and small were of no interest to buyers, and as a result, Duan stated that numerous such pieces were likely sitting in the homes of the locals. After learning about this, Dai expressed his desire to buy these "leftover" pieces at relatively high prices, and after four purchases, he obtained 126 pieces. In order to gain a clear understanding of the process of unearthing these articles, he worked on cleaning a stone coffin located on the side of the road to the primary school in Shimao. On the chest of the corpse inside, he found a fan-shaped semi-annular jade pendant, though no large jade articles were found [3].

In 1981, Zhang Changshou of the Institute of Archaeology at the Chinese Academy of Social Sciences carried out a survey of the Shimao site and saw the jade pieces collected by the locals including yazhang (rectangular ritual objects with a blade and teeth), knives, bi discs (disc-shaped articles with a hole in the middle), semi-annular pendants, axes, and battle axes. He obtained three such articles for himself [4].

That same year, the Xi'an Banpo Museum executed a test dig on a small area at the Shimao site. They discovered stone coffins and burial urns from which they collected jade, stone, and earthenware articles [5].

In 1986, another survey of the Shimao site was done by Lyu Zhirong of the Shaanxi Institute of Archaeology [6].

A number of years after Lyu's survey, agencies in Yulin City in charge of managing cultural relics and the Shenmu County Cultural Artifact Bureau successively carried out numerous surveys of the site and discovered jade articles and other relics [7].

In 2010, the Shenmu People's Government submitted a request to the Shaanxi Bureau of Relics that an expert archaeological team be sent to Shimao to carry out an excavation and salvage as much as possible. At the time, I was in charge of archaeological work at the bureau, and I signed and issued this request on that document submitted from Shenmu: "A request for the Shaanxi Provincial Institute of Archaeology to arrange an archaeological excavation as soon as possible and submit an application for excavation to the State Administration of Cultural Heritage. All expenses will first be paid by Shenmu County."

In 2011, the Shaanxi Provincial Institute of Archaeology, the Yulin Municipal Archaeological Research Team, and the Shenmu County Cultural Artifact Bureau jointly formed an excavation team to carry out a large-scale survey of the site. They discovered that the site was much larger than originally thought, and they worked with

greater attention to detail as they possessed more advanced methods and technologies. What they found exceeded their expectations by far.

After receiving approval from the State Administration of Cultural Heritage in 2012, the Shaanxi Provincial Institute of Archaeology and other agencies working in the cultural relic realm at the municipal and county levels formed another excavation team. After a few years of research and studies of unearthed artifacts, the substantial results have stunned the academic world: A massive amount of evidence shows that the site is vastly extensive, strictly ordered in its layout, complete with all the functions a society of the time would need, and rich with artifacts. In short, it is a "super" example of a prehistoric archaeological site in northern China [8].

The "Super" Neolithic City

Based on carbon-14 dating and archaeological evidence, construction on the city of Shimao began around 2300 BCE, and the city was later abandoned around 1800 BCE. It is now known to cover an area of over 4 million square meters. To date, it is currently the largest known settlement in China from the time period between the late Shimao period and the early Xia dynasty [9]. In comparison, the Liangzhu culture covered 2.9 million square meters, the mid-Taosi culture covered an area of 2.8 million square meters, and the Shijiahe culture covered an area of 1.2 million square meters. According to the latest research, if the areas containing remains directly related to yet outside the city of Shimao are included, the site could actually be said to cover 10 million square meters. Based on size alone, it is by no means an exaggeration to call the city "super."

(2) The Shimao city consists of three major components: the "Huangchengtai (royal complex platform)," inner city, and outer city. The inner and outer portions of the city were divided by 2.5-meter-thick stone walls stretching for a length of 10,000 meters. Today, the remains of the walls are about one meter high. The inner city houses the royal complex platform, and its walls are arranged in basically a northeast-to-southwest orientation, covering an area of about 2.1 million square meters. The outer city, covering about 1.9 million square meters, extends off the southeastern section of the inner wall toward the southeast with an arc-shaped wall that closes it off. The royal complex platform, about 2,000 square meters in area, was the central location of a large palace complex and exquisite buildings. There is a pond in the northern section, which, from what we can see today, is about two meters deep and covers about 300 square meters. The most fascinating aspect is that the platform is surrounded by a retaining wall of up to ten layers of stone, each layer being about three meters tall. Some of the stones in the wall have diamond-shaped eye patterns carved into them. The platform was built as a strong, well-proportioned pyramid. Near the platform, stone sculptures of human heads, alligator bones, and murals have been found. Research teams have been excavating the site of the platform gate in recent years, and it was found to contain four main components: a plaza, a barbican, piers on the northern and southern sides, and an inner barbican. There is a road at the stone platform foundation road and a retaining wall. The plaza, which covers an area of 2,100 square meters, is on the outside of the gate. Evidence shows that the royal complex platform represents the existence of a king at that time who enjoyed the highest rank among the people, and it serves as the most persuasive evidence regarding the history of early China's large cities and civilizations.

The eastern gate of the outer city is located to the northeast, facing in that direction. There are inner and outer barbicans, a gateway, piers made of stone and rammed earth, rooms to the sides, and mamian (horse face-shaped reinforcement features for defense). The discovery of such structure and layout completely overturned the prevailing ideas about the history of ancient Chinese cities. On the ground near the bottoms of stone walls built at later dates, over 300 fragments of murals have been found. The murals, geometric shapes of red, yellow, black, and orange, were painted on a white background (lime). Lyu Yufei, a researcher from Peking University, believes the eastern gate of Shimao was purposely slightly situated to the northeast so that there would be no shadow in the gateway at sunrise on the summer solstice. The overall design of the eastern gate shows the inhabitants of the city had a relatively developed understanding of astronomy.

In brief, the eastern gate of the outer city at Shimao is, to date, the earliest of all known ancient gate sites that is well-preserved, massive in scale, complex in structure, advanced in building technique, and refined in its ornamentation. Despite over 4,000 years of erosion from weather, it still possesses an air of grandeur and majesty. Located at a commanding elevation of the city, it was used to control who came and went, serving as a solid screen of defense. Thus, it is duly known as "the first gateway of the Chinese people."

(3) Three forms of burial have been found at Shimao: urns, stone coffins, and pits in the ground. Highly similar to the urns of the Yangshao culture, the urns at Shimao were mainly used for children. Stone coffins, whose use

was a result of the abundance of stone in the area, were used mainly for adolescents. But most of the graves were pits in the ground, which were used for adults. The sizes of these pit graves and types of funerary objects found within vary greatly. In Hanjia Gedan, pit graves of two square meters and larger have been found, the largest, "M1," measuring four meters in length, three in breadth, and six in depth. Over 20 jade pieces, more than 10 painted earthenware pieces, and one round piece with a semblance of teeth made of jade and gold were found in the pit [10].

(4) Mass sacrificial graves have been found buried in six areas in the outer city near the eastern gate. The number of bones in each is different, ranging from 1 to 24. After preliminary evaluations of the bones in the K1 pit, it was found that most of those who were killed en masse and buried under the earliest foundations of the walls were young women. This act may have been related to the building of the foundation or ritual while the city was being built [11].

Investigations show that the huge city of Shimao was not alone. Beginning at around 2300 BCE, settlements ranging from a few hundred to a few thousand square meters were established in the south-central part of Inner Mongolia, northern Shaanxi, and northwestern Shanxi. Nearly 100 such settlements have been found around the Shimao city area in northern Shaanxi alone, and more than ten of them were located in the Tuwei River valley (where Shimao is located). Archaeologists at Shimao have said these smaller settlements were comparable to numerous twinkling stars surrounding the bright moon (Shimao). They were secondary and tertiary centers of the Shimao kingdom, and they ensured the survival of Shimao's strong social foundation for four to five hundred years.

The Shimao site was home to a "super" stone city (complete with palace structures, exquisite buildings, altars, mass sacrificial graves, artisan workshops, residential areas, and cemeteries for the nobility) containing many stone sculptures of human heads, bronze implements, and numerous finely crafted jade implements. All of this shows that it held a large population with a hierarchical society. It had a massive yet ordered management mechanism such that the power of the society could be mobilized when needed. As Yi Hua, a member of the Dongcheng Xijiu Cultural Communications Company, has said, it was a place that magnificently transformed from a kingdom that produced jade and silk into one that produced jade dagger-axes. Without a doubt, by the time of the Xia dynasty, the Shimao kingdom had already arrived at the threshold of the civilized age.

Amazing Jade Articles

The amazing aspects of jade articles found at Shimao include the following:

First, before excavation even took place, the local villagers had found jade articles while carrying out their daily work, or they sometimes found them in holes they happened upon (not knowing the functions of these holes). Some of the locals say that jade articles could even be found in the cracks of the walls at Shimao. Since these pieces were not discovered through archaeological excavation, some experts have reservations about the villagers' stories. Moreover, some extremely discreet experts have their doubts about the dating and even authenticity of the pieces. Thus, there is not one piece of Shimao jade in the 1996 work *Complete Collection of Chinese Jade*. Apparently, the editorial committee for this book had discussed whether or not to include the pieces, but in order to avoid unnecessary controversy, they decided against it [12]. Jade articles have been found in recent years within the stone walls near the eastern gate and the royal complex platform. Whether they were found within the rubble of collapsed wall sections or found on the outer edges of the walls of the stone buildings, analysis shows they were likely placed within the walls purposely during construction. (Shaanxi Institute of Archaeology head Sun Zhouyong told me that another xuan-ji disc [an irregularly shaped jade disc with a hole in the middle] was discovered at the royal complex platform this year.) In addition to jade pieces being found within the walls, some were also found upon further excavation of graves that had already been dug into, and others were found at the altar (or watchtower, as some believe) outside the eastern section of the city. Thus, the riddle of where the Shimao jade has come from was solved [13]. Placing jade within the walls of the city and the palace is quite a unique phenomenon, evidence that the rulers of Shimao held jade as a sacred object. That is, the jade being placed within the walls was believed to enhance their power by some mysterious means, strengthening them further to defend against invasion.

Second, the types of jade articles found at Shimao are numerous and varied. There are bi discs, xuan-ji discs (yabi discs), rings, yazhang, large knives, battle-axes, cong tubes (hollow rectangular prisms), semi-annular pendants, sculptures of human heads, hairpins, and birds. Noteworthy is that the earliest-known jade dagger-axe was found there.

Third, the most unique articles found at Shimao are the large yazhang, large knives, and xuan-ji discs.

At least 100 yazhang have been found at Shimao. Besides the 28 pieces (including three that were later reworked) collected by Dai Yingxin years ago, most of them are in museums in the US, Europe, and Japan; the Shanghai Museum holds the largest collection of them still in China [14]. According to current data, the longest yazhang from Shimao is 53.5 cm. It was bought by Alfred Salmony in 1929 and is now part of the collection at the Cologne Museum of Far Eastern Art [15]. In recent years, four jade yazhang have been unearthed at Shimao. Though they are damaged, they are without question extremely valuable in an academic sense. Based on their color, quality, and shape, it is certain that most of the yazhang which are now abroad and in other parts of China originated in Shimao.

The large knives unearthed at Shimao are also great in number. Besides those at the Shaanxi History Museum, the museum with the largest collection is the Palace Museum in Beijing. Nine of these knives are part of the Compendium of Collections in the Palace Museum: Jade. Eight of them were designated as being from the Shaanxi Shimao culture, and the ninth was designated as from the Shimao culture. I believe without a doubt that all of the pieces are from the Shimao site in Shenmu, as evidenced by the aspects of material, color variance (as a result of having been buried for a long time), markings, shape, and craftsmanship. One of the knives has five holes and is 78.7 cm long, 12.8 cm wide, and 0.3 cm thick [16]. Another relatively long jade knife from Shimao was bought by Dai Yingxin. It was originally broken and registered as two different pieces, but workers at the Shaanxi History Museum happened to realize that the pieces were of the same color and thickness and that they could be joined together seamlessly, hence its later being verified as a single piece. It is 71 cm long, 11.5 cm wide at its larger end, and 0.25 cm thick. The back of the blade has four holes, and on one side of the larger end, there is decorative carving that suggests the profile of a divinity [17].

Based on incomplete data, at least 100 xuan-ji discs have also been found at Shimao. They come in a number of shapes, and most of them were crafted impeccably from high-quality jade.

Regarding craftsmanship, the jade pieces at Shimao are large and thin, especially the yazhang, some of which are even as thin as paper at less than two millimeters. A few of them only weigh 30 – 50 grams, feeling as though they could break while being held in your palm. For the Shimao artisans to have produced such refined and large yet thin jade instruments 4,000 years ago, it is obvious they were highly skilled.

Fourth, among the many articles of jade unearthed at Shimao, besides those made by local artisans, cong tubes (reworked) from the Liangzhu culture, tiger heads and eagle-shaped hairpins from the Shijiahe culture, and cong tubes and bi discs from the Qijia culture have been found there. This shows that the Shimao culture was either powerful or that its rulers were tolerant and accepting of things from other cultures.

Fifth, where exactly were the jade articles of Shimao crafted? While it is obvious that the pieces from the Liangzhu, Shijiahe, and Qijia cultures were not made in Shimao, the refined yazhang, knives, and xuan-ji discs typical of the area were certainly made locally. Nonetheless, some scholars believe that the yazhang found at Shimao were actually stolen from the Shijiahe culture [18]. This idea lacks sufficient evidence and is a misinterpretation of what

happened.

Sixth, many jade artifacts unearthed at Shimao are made of various types of jade. A small portion of them are white jade, and there are also greenish-white and greenish-yellow pieces. The majority of yazhang and large knives (which are the highlights from Shimao) were made of a relatively unique type of black jade. The expert Deng Shuping believes that before its obvious deterioration, this type of jade had aggradation-produced lines in clumps or wavy lines. After analyzing samples of this sort of jade, professor Wen Guang verified that it was formed by very small, densely accumulated crystallites. This explains why the jade could be made into large, thin articles that are not apt to chip. Deng applied the technological methods used by Chen Donghe on the Shimao jade pieces at the Musée Guimet in France to discover that there is a relatively high concentration of ferric ions, manganese, and nickel, and as a result, Deng proposed that the Shimao culture discovered this dark nephrite (rich in iron and manganese) in northern Shaanxi, finding it to be useful in making especially thin and sharp yet strong yazhang and long knives with holes [19].

Jade Collection of the Shenmu County Shimao Culture Research Society

The loss of jade articles from Shimao began at the latest during the late Qing dynasty, and a large number of pieces were lost during the Republic of China period as well. A number of museums in other countries have jade pieces from Shimao. Some were sold as raw jade to be made into new jade articles during the Cultural Revolution, accounting for a huge loss. Dai Yingxin's contribution years ago to collecting pieces must not go unrecognized. The loss has also been severe over the past ten years or so. While it is true the locals are accidentally finding pieces, there are also greedy people who took advantage of the lack of monitoring in the area and carried out illegal digs. For the people of Shenmu County and for the love of his hometown, Hu Wengao has been involved at Shimao since the 1990s. Because of his job, he came to know firsthand that locals had ancient jade, earthenware, and stone implements in their homes, and many of these pieces had already made their way into the hands of so-called "collectors" in places such as Beijing, Shanghai, Shanxi, and Henan. This was quite a disappointment for Hu, and it triggered in him the idea of buying up the ancient relics there. Thus, he applied for the establishment of the Shenmu County Shimao Culture Research Society, and for over 20 years, he has invested greatly into buying back jade articles unearthed at Shimao from collectors all over. Items he collects include ancient earthenware, stone, and jade pieces from Shimao, and he has so far collected over 1,000, about 100 of them being jade. His research society has held to this foundational principle since its inception: pieces collected are absolutely not to be resold for profit. The only objective of the society is to keep the cultural roots of Shenmu in Shenmu, and to provide these pieces to scholars for the sake of research. Thousands of Chinese and foreign archaeology scholars, as well as people from various other sectors, have come to carry out observation and research at the society. Moreover, nearly 100 well-reputed scholars from institutions involved in the research of ancient Chinese jade have been invited by the society to participate in seminars and discuss these reclaimed pieces.

Hu's society also has as its vision to build a museum open to the public in the near future. Some may think that keeping these articles in the walls, altars, and graves to be discovered by archaeologists is a beautiful thing, and their scientific value would naturally be very high. This would be the most ideal condition, but it is not the reality. If we removed ourselves from the background of reality and explored the right and wrong involved, we would be unable to reach a fact-based conclusion. The reason for the loss of jade articles from Shimao since the 1980s is, first, that their importance was unknown: the locals merely knew that there happened to be numerous jade articles there, and that such articles could be sold for a small profit; they had no idea of what era the articles came from or what they had been used for. Also, it was commonly known that the Shimao site is quite remote, vast, hard to access with its roads winding through the hills, sparsely populated, and had neither a custodial institution nor any cultural preservation workers supervising activity there. Thus, preservation was extremely difficult from an objective point of view. Moreover, Shenmu County is rich in premium-quality coal. Since the Reform and Opening Up, a great number of people have invested in coal mining and become billionaires there, whereas the number of people who care about and invest in collecting these ancient relics is quite small. After years of relentless work, running around, spending time and money, the Shenmu County Shimao Culture Research Society has finally allowed for most of the jade found in Shenmu to stay there. All of this has been for the sake of being able to study the highly precious resources found at the Shimao site; otherwise, these important relics would be lost, and we would no longer be able to see the jade articles of Shimao in their truest form. It is for this reason that the work of Hu and his society cannot go unrecognized and is extremely worthy of affirmation.

Of the jade pieces in the society's collection, even though there are no yazhang yet, there are quite a lot of other forms: besides the numerous bi discs, there are also high-collared bi discs, xuan-ji discs (yabi discs), three-component xuan-ji discs, and high-collared xuan-ji discs. The jade cong tubes are divided into the categories of tall and short, most of which are undecorated. There are also tiered cong tubes and cong tubes from the Liangzhu culture that have been cut and reworked. A majority of the semi-annular pendants are arced and have narrow bodies, though there are also some which are fan-shaped. In addition, there are many battle-axes, knives, and handle-shaped implements. There are also a number of jade pendants in the shapes of animals such as silkworms, fish, frogs, snakes, and birds. Even though they are not completely realistic, they capture vividly the features of the profile of the animal intended. For example, there are two birds standing back to back on one piece with their profile outlines protruding while other parts have been hollowed out. It seems simple, yet it has quite a lifelike feel. Another pendant has a bird with its head turned as if it were looking back, and it is situated atop a group of birds connected to each other at the bottom. Also on this piece are a cross and a hollowed-out, symmetrical "£"-shaped design. The highly artistic expression exhibits a truly full sense of life. The most fascinating pieces are the many yabi discs, which are varied in shape and exquisite in craftsmanship. One bi disc is as thin as paper and has been polished to the highest degree of brightness, leaving those who view it unable to believe their eyes. One bracelet-shaped piece is inscribed with extremely fine lines which

are difficult to see unless it is viewed from the side, though the pattern is in the Liangzhu style. However, the quality of the jade is exceptionally rich, and its color and quality make it seem different from Liangzhu jade, which means there are two possibilities for its background: either a Shimao artisan copied the Liangzhu style, or it was first made by a Liangzhu artisan before being further worked by a Shimao artisan. I hold to the latter theory. Even though we see extremely fine patterning on jade yazhang and knives from Shimao, they are usually of straight lines or lines crossing at an incline; to date, Liangzhu-style curved line patterning has yet to be found at Shimao, and the color and quality of the jade are different. I believe that the same jade article buried in the soil of the southern Taihu Lake basin area and in the soil of the Loess Plateau would naturally look different after 4,000 years.

In a word, the jade articles of the Shenmu County Shimao Culture Research Society are rich in variety, and most of them are of high-quality jade crafted with refined skill. For those who wish to learn more about the jade articles of Shimao, the collection is a rare and invaluable treasure.

The Shimao site of today has already been declared by the State Council as a Key Historic Site under State Protection. The local government and cultural management agencies of all levels now have a new consciousness of the importance of this site. The local government has established a vice-county level agency in charge of the preservation of cultural relics. The standing committee of the Shaanxi People's Congress formulated and issued the *Shimao Site Preservation Regulations*, and as a result, local people and officials alike have gained a heightened awareness of the law regarding the preservation of cultural relics. In this way, the loss of historical artifacts from the Shimao site that occurred throughout history will no longer take place. With continued archaeological excavation, a number of indicators have already been found to show the ancient civilization that existed around 4,000 years ago on the Loess Plateau will continue to produce surprising secrets.

Notes:

[1] Fan Peiwei. *On the History of Gaojiapu*. Shaanxi People's Publishing House, Shaanxi Xinhua Publishing and Media Group, 2015. From the 1958 Shenmu County archives.

[2] Sun Zhouyong, and Shao Jing. Discovering Shimao Ancient City, "Shimao: Past, Present, and Future." ,Cultural Relics Press, 2016, p.9. Once the Site Registry was completed from the survey of Shimao, An Zhimin entrusted it to the care of Gong Qiming.

[3] Dai Yingxin. "Recollections of Excavations at and Jade Articles from the Shimao Site." *Collection World*, Issues 5 and 6, 2014.

[4] Zhang Changshou. *On the Excavation and Knife-shaped Blades Unearthed at the Shimao Site in Shenmu County*, and *Studies on Ancient Culture in Southern China and Nearby Regions*, Chinese University Press, 1994.

[5] Xi'an Banpo Museum. "Briefing on Survey and Test Dig at Shimao Site of Shenmu County, Shaanxi." *Prehistory*, Issue 2, 1983. Wei Shigang, "Stories about Dig at Shimao Site of Shenmu County, Shaanxi." *Prehistory 2000, San Qin Publishing House*

[6] Lyu Zhirong. "Microliths Found at Shimao Site of Shenmu County, Shaanxi." *Wenbo*, Issue 2, 1989.

[7] Sun Zhouyong, and Shao Jing. Discovering Shimao Ancient City, "Shimao: Past, Present, and Future.", Cultural Relics Press, 2016, p.9.

[8] Shaanxi Provincial Institute of Archaeology, Yulin Municipal Archaeological Research Team, and Shenmu County Cultural Artifact Bureau. "Shimao Site of Shenmu County, Shaanxi." *Archaeology*, Issue 7, 1983.

[9] See 8.

[10] Shao Jing. "Shimao Site." *Annual Report of Shaanxi Provincial Institute of Archaeology*, 2014.

[11] See 8

[12] *Complete Collection of Chinese Jade*. Hebei Fine Arts Publishing House, 1996. I was informed of the information by ,Yang Boda, editor-in-chief of this book.

[13] Sun Zhouyong, and Shao Jing. "A Few Problems Regarding the Background of Jade Articles Unearthed at Shimao." Spirit of Jade, Soul of China—Collected Academic Seminars on Ancient Chinese Jade Articles and Traditional Culture (6), Zhejiang Ancient Books Publishing House, 2011.

[14] Minao Hayashi. *Studies on Ancient Chinese Jade*

Articles. Translated by Yang Meili, Art Book Co., Ltd., 1997, p. 330, images 6 – 99.

[15] From the conference *Yazhang in East Asia* held in Zhengzhou in late 2016, in which Zhang Wei spoke about 12 Shimao yazhang that are part of the Shanghai Museum collection.

[16] Palace Museum editorial board. *Compendium of Articles in the Palace Museum Collection: Jade Articles 1*. Neolithic Era. Forbidden City Press and Anhui Fine Arts Publishing House, 2011.

[17] This piece was originally registered as two pieces: SSY83 and SSY117.

[18] The idea that this yazhang was stolen is held by Professor Guo Jingyun at Taiwan's National Chung Cheng University. This proposal can be seen in: "My Opinion on the Origins of the Yazhang and the Riddle of the Jade Articles from Northern Shaanxi." *Journal of China Three Gorges University*, Humanities and Social Sciences ed., Volume 36, Issue 5, 2014.

[19] Deng Shuping. "A Reconsideration of Four Jade Articles Unearthed at Yangjiabu, the Jin Hou Tomb, and Lushanmao." *The East and Its Jade—Dawenkou Shimao. Cultural Exhibition of Liangzhu Jade Articles*, Cultural Relics Press, 2014, pp.13 – 32.

石峁玉器观感

古 方

陕西神木市石峁文化研究会（前称"神木龙山文化研究会"）所藏的一批石峁玉器，数量众多，种类丰富，长期以来颇受学术界关注[1]。笔者仔细观摩了本书所刊布的近300件石峁玉器，拟就这批玉器的造型、纹饰、玉质、雕工及沁色等问题进行初步的探讨。

一、石峁玉器器型

主要有璧、联璜璧、环、璇玑、璜、斧、钺、锛、刀、圭、琮、镯、柄形器、佩饰（串饰）、工具等。

1. 璧环类：扁平圆形，中央有孔，表面光素无纹，依孔径大小分为璧与环。此类为石峁玉器主项之一，约占玉器总数五分之一。璧、环的中孔均为正圆形（图1），孔壁圆滑，但有的外缘并非正圆形，有切割截取、打钻和沁蚀残缺的痕迹（图2）。有的环体上留有钻孔，并镶嵌绿松石小圆片（图3）。有的环内孔边缘两面凸起，亦称"有领环"或"突缘环"（图4）。

2. 璜及联璜璧环类：扁平弧形，呈半圆或扇面状，表面光素无纹，大多两端有孔（图5）。此类也包括一些不规则的璜形器。两件以上的璜组合起来

图1

图2

图3

图 4

图 5

图 6

图 7

图 8-1

图 8-2

即形成联璜璧或环，有双联和三联两种形态。将璧或环一分为二为双联，三等分为三联（图 6）。璜之间有孔相对，可穿线编连起来。有的联璜璧环并非有意为之，而是无意间璧、环破裂后，再穿孔将破裂处缀合所形成的。

3. 琮：呈外方内圆状。有两种形态：一种琮体呈方柱形，素面，为同时代的齐家文化玉琮风格（图 7）。另一种琮体做出四个角部，一般饰有平行刻线将每个角部三等分，或者在转角处对称刻两个小圆圈，象征人面或兽面，明显是仿自时代较早的良渚文化神人兽面纹玉琮的样式（图 8-1、2）。亦有少量的琮形器，可能是半成品或琮的余料。

4. 镯：扁圆筒状或筒状。以扁圆筒状居多，一般为素面（图 9）。有的表面刻等分竖槽或附有四个凸块，具有良渚玉琮的特征（图 10）。筒状镯呈直筒状或束腰状，素面或饰凹弦纹。

5. 斧钺刀类：扁平长方形，刃部略长于背部，近背部有穿孔。此类亦称端刃形器，为石峁玉器数量最多的一类，约占玉器总数三分之一。需要说明的是，以前描述石峁玉器时，多提到"玉铲"一

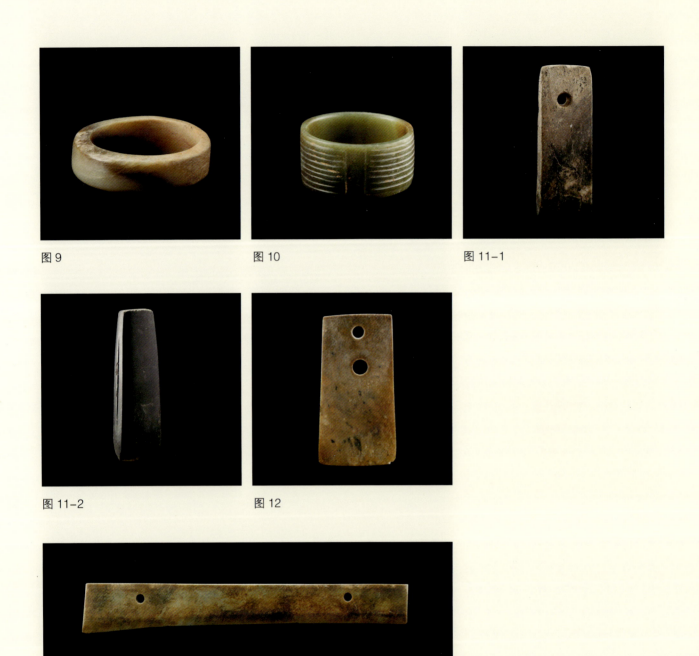

图 9

图 10

图 11-1

图 11-2

图 12

图 13

词，实际上应归到斧钺一类。斧体厚重，有使用痕迹，有的无孔，应为手斧（图 11-1、2）。钺体较薄，制作较精细（图 12）。斧钺的刃部有直刃和弧刃两种，双面磨刃，近背部多有一孔，亦有两孔者，其中一

孔似为后补或由其他带孔玉器改制而来。刀有长短之分，短者似为斧钺改制而成，即将斧钺一侧边磨出刃，而保留有原刃；长者呈长条状，刃内弧，一侧边常磨出刃，纵视似斧钺，近背部有 2-4 孔不等，

有齐家文化玉刀特征(图13)。另外,还有少量的戈、矛等,忽略不论。

6. 璇玑:又称牙璧,扁平圆形中有孔,外缘雕刻三牙(极少四牙),似风车状(图14)。亦有用联璜璧和高领环改制的(图15)。有的在牙之间雕出一至三组不等的扉棱。少数璇玑近长方形,四角出牙,与山西清凉寺庙底沟二期遗址出土璇玑相似,有原始风格(图16)。有的璇玑与带齿铜环同出,表面遗留有铜锈痕迹,应该是配套使用的(图17-1、2)。还有一种璇玑形环,环体外缘刻有三至四组扉棱(图18),或许是模仿带齿铜环的样式。

7. 柄形器:扁平长条形,顶端似蘑菇形,末端未加修饰,应嵌又有漆木器一类的柄状物(图19)。柄形器盛行于商晚期,而石峁出土的柄形器应该是最早的实例之一,它可能是某一部落成员身份的标识物品,类似今天的身份证。

8. 佩饰:包括一些穿孔小型玉饰、玉簪首、玉管、各种质料的串饰等。玉饰中可辨出形象的有人、鸟、鱼、蛇、蝉等,其中最重要的是一件侧面人

图 14

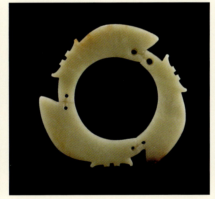

图 15

图 16

图 17-1

图 17-2

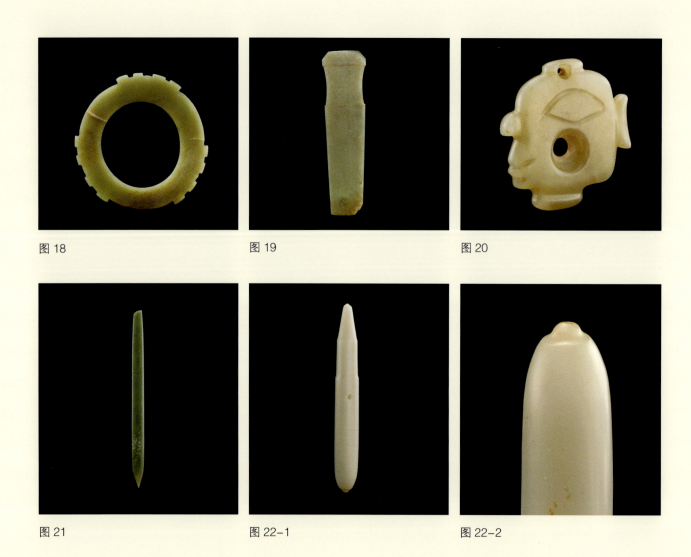

图 18　　　　　　　　　　图 19　　　　　　　　　　图 20

图 21　　　　　　　　　　图 22-1　　　　　　　　　图 22-2

头像，大眼垂耳鹰钩鼻，脸上有一穿孔，造型与上世纪七十年代在石峁遗址征集的一件极为相似（图 20）。

9、工具主要是玉刻刀和玉钻头。玉刻刀柄部细长，一端呈尖锥状（图 21）。有一部分是用石家河文化的鹰首玉簪改制而成。在粗大的一端磨出乳突状的钻头，另一端保持原有的榫头状，用以嵌插钻杆。由于长期使用和摩擦，有的钻头已磨秃，原有纹饰也漫漶不清（图 22-1、2）。

二、石峁玉器玉质与工艺

总体来看，斧、钺、刀等玉质很杂，有透闪石、阳起石、石英岩、大理岩、蛇纹石化大理岩等，硬度和透明度不一，纹理较粗，杂质和绺裂多，显示出较复杂的玉色，多呈灰色、青色、绿色、褐色、黑色。一件玉器上还可见几种混杂的颜色。璧、环和璇玑的玉质较好，基本上为透闪石，较纯净，有蜡质光泽，特别是璇玑用料较精，温润细腻。玉色以黄绿色、绿色、青白色为主。

石峁玉器的沁色较少，大多可见玉质。一些玉器局部有沁色，一种为土沁，呈灰白或灰褐色（图23）；另一种为深浅不一的褐色（咖啡色），为含铁元素沁蚀所致。在这种沁色上往往有发散出一种灰黄色沁，这种沁色也常见于齐家文化玉器上（图24）。

石峁玉器工艺特点有：1. 切割。开料切割技术比较成熟，切割面很平整。以片切割为主，常留下对切的错位痕迹，偶见线切割痕迹。锯的厚度最薄仅1~2毫米（图25），推测当时已使用金属直条锯（石峁遗址已出土青铜刀和石范），而且稳定性相当好，或许已有简单的车床式机械。2. 钻孔。有实心钻和空心钻两种。实心钻用于钻斧、钺、刀、璜上较小的孔，单面钻成（图26）。空心钻用于钻璧、环、璇玑及玉刀上较大的孔，均为单面钻成（图27）。单面钻会留下上大下小喇叭形钻孔痕迹，这是龙山晚期普遍的现象。但石峁玉璧、环和璇玑有一种独特的修孔现象，即将中孔两端的角部打磨掉（俗称"倒棱"），使孔壁变得圆滑（图28）。3. 常见剖片和改制现象。所谓剖片，是将一件片状玉器从侧面横向或平面纵向一剖为二，切割面不做任何

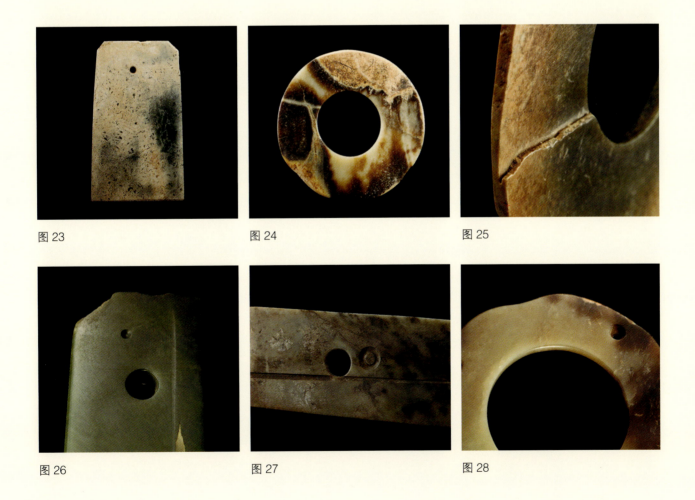

图 23　　　　　　　　图 24　　　　　　　　图 25

图 26　　　　　　　　图 27　　　　　　　　图 28

图 29

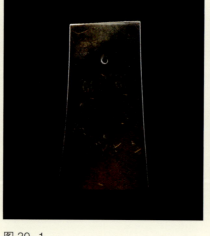

图 30-1

图 30-2

图 31-1

图 31-2

打磨和抛光，常见有一剖为二，或二剖为四，最多见四剖为八者（图29）。这样做既保持了原器的形状，又使玉器数量成倍增加。所谓改制，是将一件玉器切割改为其他的器型。例如，有两件玉钺就是用一件玉璋分割而成的，其中一件尚留有璋的扉棱和阴刻线的痕迹（图30-1、2）。还有一件玉镯是用良渚文化神人兽面纹玉琮横向切割而成，从遗留的纹饰来看，这件玉琮被分割成了4件玉镯（图31-1、2）。综上所述，石峁制玉工艺中裁截和分割技术很发达。值得一提的是，在一些玉器发现了砣具琢刻的痕迹，即琢刻痕呈梭形，砣线两端有细密的放射状划痕（俗称"跑刀"或"出刀"）（图32-1、2）。

三、余论

我们对石峁玉器的认识是有一个漫长过程的。石峁玉器传世历史可上溯至清代晚期。1872~1876

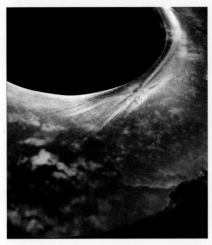

图 32-1

图 32-2

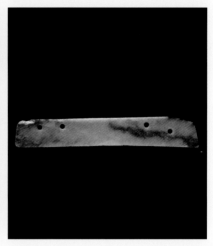

图 33

图 34

年吴大澂在西安任职陕甘学政的时候，所收藏的玉器大部分为陕北出土的玉刀、玉璋、玉璧、玉环、璇玑等器物。吴氏藏玉中有 28 件现藏于加拿大皇家安大略博物馆，其中玉刀（编号 928.12.81，图 33）和璇玑（编号 928.12.57，图 34）与本图录同类器物极为相似[2]。民国时期是中国文物外流的高峰期，石峁玉器也不例外，大量流入欧美一些学术机构和博物馆，尤以美国最多[3]。在早期的玉器研究中，石峁玉器无疑扮演了重要的角色。由于石峁玉器大多体形较大且呈几何形，造型与古文献记述的礼器近似，故吴大澂认为它们是三代礼器，并依《周礼》等经书对它们的定名和用途进行了详细的考证，其研究成果发表于 1889 年成书的《古玉图考》中[4]。在美国，西方研究中国玉器的开拓者贝特霍尔德·劳费尔（Berthold Laufer）非常欣赏吴大澂的考证，在他 1912 年出版的《玉器：中国考古学和宗教学研究》一书中，几乎全盘引用吴大澂对玉礼器的描述[5]。有意思的是，劳费尔在书中宣称，中国没有史前时代，也没有新石器时代或者制造使用石器的时代。当时考古学在中国还没有诞生，这样荒谬的论述是不足为奇的。20 世纪初，中国早期玉器在西方被发展成一种收藏品和被寻求的物品，这应该主要归功于劳费尔。他不仅在学术上积极向西方受众介绍中国早期玉器，而且对中国玉器有着

图 35-1

图 35-2

狂热的喜爱[6]。在他的影响下，美国重要的中国文物收藏家不但收藏有石峁玉器，如佛利尔（Charles Lang Freer）、桑尼辰（Edward Sonnenschein）、温索浦（Grenvill L. Winthrop）、皮尔斯白瑞（Alfred F. Pillsbury）、韩美林（Chauncy Hamlin）、德鲁蒙德（Wyman Drummond）和赛克勒（Arthur M. Sackler）等，而且这些玉器在博物馆展览中居于醒目的位置。当然也是由于劳费尔出版的著作风行欧美，使得吴大澂和其《古玉图考》在海外名声大作，以至于"吴大澂玉器"做为一个品牌让海外藏家趋之若鹜，一求先睹为快[7]。

直到上世纪七十年代前，传世的石峁玉器器类以牙璋、斧、钺、刀为主，这是因为它们来自当地农民掘城墙寻找的玉器，以及平整土地过程中偶见的祭祀坑玉器（图 35-1，箭头所指之处为一处祭祀坑位置；图 35-2，从该祭祀坑位置遥望东门遗址）。但这些玉器的具体出土地点无人知晓。1976 年戴应新先生到石峁遗址调查并征集到百余件玉器，初步

认定了玉器出土地点及时代，从此揭开了石峁玉器的神秘面纱[8]。自九十年代以来，石峁城址土坑墓大量出土的璧、环和璇玑逐渐为世人所知。据粗略统计，海内外文博考古机构及私人收藏石峁玉器总数量约 3000~4000 左右[9]。

从目前掌握的信息来看，石峁玉器主要出土于石砌城墙或建筑基址、祭祀坑（或窖藏）和大型土坑墓。石砌城墙或建筑基址出土的玉器以原器或对剖的斧、钺、刀、璋为代表；祭祀坑以璋、钺、刀为代表；土坑墓以环类和璇玑为代表。

1996~1999 年神木新华遗址玉器坑和 2011 年以来石峁遗址的考古发掘，出土了不少玉器，为石峁玉器的准确断代提供了依据。新华遗址距石峁遗址约 20 公里，文化面貌一致。其玉器坑（K1）出土玉器 36 件，器形有玉钺、玉铲、玉刀、玉斧、玉环、玉璜、玉璋等，分 6 排竖直侧立插入土中，器物之间基本平行。新华遗存的年代在公元前 2150~前 1900 年之间，其下限已进入夏纪年[10]在石峁外城

东门的发掘清理中共出土玉器21件，有玉铲、玉璋、玉璜、玉刀、玉锛等，大多数器物出土位置明确，为了解石峁玉器的埋藏情况提供了重要线索[11]。

石峁遗址的遗存分为早晚两期，即龙山晚期（公元前2300~前2200年）和夏初年（公元前2000~前1900年）[12]。实际上，我们目前见到的石峁玉器基本上属于夏初年的，那么石峁遗址中龙山晚期的玉器面貌究竟是什么样的？与夏初年的玉器有什么区别？这恐怕要靠今后更多的考古发掘资料去解答。

什么是石峁玉器中具有特色的器物？这是一个不太容易回答的问题。因为石峁玉器中大部分也见于同时期其他文化的玉器品种或早于石峁时期的玉器，比如璧、环、牙璋、斧、钺、刀、琮等主要器类，也常见于齐家文化和陶寺文化玉器中。如果用两种器物来作为石峁玉器的代表，那就是璇玑和牙璋。石峁的璇玑玉质好，数量多，样式丰富，是同时代其他文化所没有的。更重要的是它与带齿铜环

图36

同出，配套使用，具有某种固定的宗教用途，对于认识和研究石峁先民的精神世界有重要的意义。牙璋的研究在学术界是热门课题之一，论证繁多，不再赘述。这两种玉器的起源应该在石峁，进而传播于中原及江南。石峁玉器还反映出当时各地部落之间物质交流是比较频繁的，比如本书收录的与齐家文化或陶寺文化玉器风格一致的玉璧、玉琮、玉刀等，良渚文化玉琮、红山文化玉蝉，以及石家河文化的透雕玉饰（图36）、鹰形簪首等。以神木石峁、新华遗址为代表的玉器风格，存在于陕北及相邻的内蒙古南部地区，被称为"河套地区玉器传统"[13]。笔者曾认为，这一地区西邻齐家文化，东接陶寺文化，形成一个辽阔的玉文化分布区，而时代上正好与"玉石之路"形成阶段相吻合，是探讨"玉石之路"起源与发展的重要佐证[14]。

最后一个问题：酷爱玉器的石峁先民哪里去了？这是一个很有意思的问题，我们不妨推测一下。石峁城在当时并不是孤立的，陕晋交界的黄河两岸分布大大小小近百个石城聚落，其考古学文化面貌是一致的。这些众星拱月般环绕在石峁遗址周边的"卫星村落或次级中心"奠定了"石峁王权国家"固若磐石的存在了四五百年之久的社会基础，最终形成了以石峁遗址为代表的早期国家[15]。有趣的是，包括石峁城在内的这些石城聚落的废弃时代几乎是一样的，从石峁东城门址和皇城台遗址的发掘来看，当时城内建筑并没有受到战争的破坏，没有火烧或墙倒屋塌的痕迹（图37-1、2）。人们是主动、和平地放弃了城址，有序地撤离了石峁。石峁城内外历年来出土大型玉器的埋藏坑，可能与祭祀无关，而

图 37-1

图 37-2

是人们在撤离时，将无法带走的大型玉器匆匆掩埋。这一点在新华遗址玉器坑（K1）反映得尤其明显。该坑平面呈长方形，两短边弧凸，两长边略向内凹呈近亚腰形。长 1.40、宽 0.45~0.50、深 0.12~0.22 米，坑壁未经进一步加工，显得较为粗糙，个别地方略有坍塌损毁，坑底平整光滑，似乎是临时匆忙随意而为[16]。

是什么动力驱使石峁先民们带着神圣的玉器依依不舍离开雄伟壮观的石峁城呢？原因就是中原夏王朝的建立。安徽蚌埠禹会村的考古发掘，第一次证实了古史传说中"禹会诸侯于涂山"的真实性[17]。这个事件的影响首先是部落联盟的盟主地位由禅让制变为世袭制，禹子启建立夏王朝；其次是龙山晚期以来持续了两三百年的部落兼并运动告一段落，

各主要部落臣服于禹。禹随后分天下为九州，九州应该是行政区划。统治者治理天下最有效的手段之一就是将原住民迁徙到其他地区，进行统一管理。由此我们可以推测，从大禹开始，到夏启及其继任者，对天下部落进行迁徙，异地治之，当然石峁城也不例外。从玉器发展来看，牙璋、玉刀等器型逐渐被玉戈、柄形器等代表等级地位和身份的器型所替代。石峁先民离开故土，去往哪里恐怕是一个历史之谜了。代表夏文化的河南二里头文化遗物中仍可见到少量的牙璋和玉刀[18]，可视为石峁玉器在中原夏朝腹地的最后孑遗。牙璋的生命力似乎很强，在中原消失后继而向中国西南地区和东南沿海传播，直至西周时期。我们或可将牙璋扩散的遗迹视作石峁先民以及后裔迁播的路线。

注解：

[1] 王炜林、孙周勇：《石峁玉器的年代及相关问题》，《考古与文物》2011 年第 4 期。孙

周勇、邵晶：《关于石峁玉器出土背景的几个问题》，载《玉魂国魄——中国古代玉器

与传统文化学术讨论会文集（六）》，浙江出版社，2014 年。

[２] 沈辰、古方：《加拿大皇家安大略博物馆藏中国古代玉器》，文物出版社，2016 年。图012、023。

[３] 江伊莉、古方：《玉器时代——美国博物馆藏中国早期玉器》，科学出版社，2009 年。

[４] 吴大澂：《古玉图考》，上海同文书局刻本，1889 年。

[５] Berthold Laufer: Jade, A Study in Chinese Archaeology and Religion, Chicago: Field Museum of Natural History, 1912.

[６] 江伊莉：《20 世纪早期美国的中国古玉收藏家》，载于《玉器时代——美国博物馆藏中国早期玉器》，江伊莉、古方著，科学出版社，2009 年。

[７] 沈辰：《多生还得此相逢：吴大澂和他的藏玉》苏州博物馆编：《梅景传家——清代苏州吴氏的收藏》译林出版社，2017 年。

[８] 戴应新：A《陕西神木县石峁龙山文化遗址调查》，《考古》1977 年第 2 期。B《神木石峁龙山文化玉器》，《考古与文物》1988 年第 5、6 期。C《神木石峁龙山文化玉器探索（一～六）》，《故宫文物月刊》总 125-130 期，1993 年第 8-12 期、1994 年第 1 期。

[９] 孙周勇、邵晶：《关于石峁玉器出土背景的几个问题》，载《玉魂国魄——中国古代玉器与传统文化学术讨论会文集（六）》，浙江出版社，2014 年。

[10] 陕西省考古研究院、榆林市文物保护研究所：《神木新华》，科学出版社，2005 年。孙周勇：《神木新华遗址出土玉器的几个问题》，《中原文物》2002 年第 5 期。

[11] 孙周勇、邵晶：《关于石峁玉器出土背景的几个问题》，载《玉魂国魄——中国古代玉器与传统文化学术讨论会文集（六）》，浙江出版社，2014 年。

[12] 孙周勇、邵晶：《关于石峁玉器出土背景的几个问题》，载《玉魂国魄——中国古代玉器与传统文化学术讨论会文集（六）》，浙江出版社，2014 年。

[13] 王炜林、孙周勇：《石峁玉器的年代及相关问题》，《考古与文物》2011 年第 4 期。

[14] 古方：《对玉石之路形成时间和路线的一些认识》，《考古与文物》2004 年增刊。

[15] 孙周勇、邵晶：《石峁：过去、现在与未来》，载于《发现石峁古城》，陕西省考古研究院、榆林市文物考古勘探工作队、神木县文体广电局、神木县石峁遗址管理处编著，文物出版社，2016 年。

[16] 陕西省考古研究院、榆林市文物保护研究所：《神木新华》，科学出版社，2005 年。

[17] 中国社会科学院考古研究所、安徽省蚌埠市博物馆编著：《蚌埠禹会村》，科学出版社，2013 年。

[18] 中国社会科学院考古研究所：《偃师二里头》，中国大百科全书出版社，1999 年。

ESSAY II

ON JADE ARTICLES FROM THE SHIMAO SITE

Gu Fang

The jade articles from the Shimao site in the collection of the Shenmu County Shimao Culture Research Society, Shaanxi Province (previous Society of Longshan Culture of Shenmu County) have long been known for the large quantity and variety and attracted great interests from the academic circles [1]. The author has made a close observation on the nearly 300 jades, the photos of which are published in this book, and is to make a preliminary investigation into the shape, pattern and design, texture, craftsmanship and impregnation of the jades.

I. Shimao Site yielded jades such as *bi* pendants, joint *huang*-semicircular pendants, rings, *xuan-ji* pendants, *huang*-semicircular pendants, axes, battle-axes, adzes, knives, *gui* tablets, *cong* pieces, bracelets, handle-shaped pieces, accessories (stringed) and implements.

1. *Bi* pendants and rings: Such a piece is usually a plain round flat piece of jade with a hole in its center. It depends on the size of the hole in the center whether a piece is a *bi* pendant or ring. They are one of the major types of Shimao jades and account for about one fifth in number. Be it a *bi* pendant or ring, the hole in its center is round-shaped (Fig.1) and smooth-walled. But in some cases, the outer edge of a piece is not perfectly round, with the trace of cutting, piercing or impregnation defect (Fig.2). The body of a ring may be pierced and inlaid with calaite discs (Fig.3). The hole in the center of a ring may bulge on both sides. Such a ring is

Fig.1

Fig.2

Fig.3

Fig.4 Fig.5 Fig.6

Fig.7 Fig.8-1 Fig.8-2

known as a "collared ring" or "edged ring" (Fig.4).

2. *Huang*-semicircular pendants and joint *huang*-semicircular pendants: Such a piece is a plain flat curve in semicircular or fan shape and there are usually holes on both ends (Fig.5). This type includes irregular-shaped *huang* pieces. Two or more *huang*-semicircular pendants are joined into a joint *huang*-semicircular pendant or ring. There are dual- and triple-*huang* joint piece: bisecting a *bi* pendant or ring to get a dual-*huang* joint piece and trisecting a *bi* pendant or ring to get a triple-*huang* joint piece (Fig.6). There are holes on a *huang*-semicircular pendant through which two or more pendants are threaded. Some joint *huang*-semicircular pendants were

not designed ones; instead, they were formed by a bi pendant or ring through piercing and threading.

3. *Cong* pieces: *Cong* is a long hollow piece with rectangular sides and round inside. There are two types. One type is of a square cylinder shape and plain surfaced. It is of the style of jade *cong* of contemporaneous Qijia Culture (Fig.7). The other type features four corners on the body. Each corner is usually trisected by parallel lines, or symmetrically carved with two small circles, symbolizing a human or animal mask. This type is evidently an imitation of the *cong* with immortal being and animal mask patterns of earlier Liangzhu Culture (Fig.8-1, 2). There are some *cong*-shaped pieces that may

Fig.9   Fig.10   Fig.11-1

Fig.11-2   Fig.12

be semi-finished *cong* pieces or waste chips.

　　4. Bracelets: A bracelet is a flat cylindrical or cylindrical piece. There are more flat cylindrical ones and they are generally plain surfaced (Fig.9). A bracelet may be carved with vertical slots with equal intervals or attached with four bumps. This is of the style of a *cong* piece from Liangzhu Culture (Fig.10). A cylindrical bracelet is straight or wasp-waisted, with a plain surface or decorated with string pattern.

　　5. Axes, battle-axes and knives: Such a piece is of a flat rectangular shape. The edge is slightly longer than the back. There is a hole near the back. Such a piece is

also known as end-edge piece. This type is of the largest number in Shimao jades and takes up about one third of all the jades unearthed. It is noteworthy that "jade spades" in the past articles about the jade unearthed from Shimao Site are actually one of this type. An axe is heavy-bodied and with traces of use. There are no holes in some axes. In that case, it may be an adze (Fig.11-1, 2). A battle-axe is comparatively thin in body and of fine craftsmanship (Fig.12). Be it an axe or battle-axe, it is double-edged and the edge is straight or curved. There is usually a hole near the back. In some cases, there are two holes. In a case of two holes, one of the two seems to be pierced later than the other or the piece was remade from a pierced jade piece. Knives vary in length. A short knife seems to be remade from an axe or battle-axe; that is, one side of the axe or battle-axe was sharpened into edge and the original edge was preserved. A long knife is of a long-bar shape. The edge curves inwards. One side is usually the edge. A long knife looks like an axe or battle-axe seen from the top. There are 2-4 holes near the back. It is of the style of a jade knife from Qijia Culture (Fig.13). In addition, there are a small number of dagger-axes and spears, which will not be discussed here.

6. *Xuan-ji* pendants: Such a piece is alternatively called toothed bi pendant, which is generally carved with three (or rarely-seen four) teeth on the outer edge and looks like a pinwheel (Fig.14). A *xuan-ji* pendant may be remade from a joint *huang*-semicircular pendant or collared ring (Fig.15). In some cases, there are 1-3 groups of protruding edges between teeth. A small number of *xuan-ji* pendants are nearly of a rectangular shape, with teeth on the four corners. Such a piece looks similar to the *xuan-ji* pendant unearthed from Miaodigou Phase II Site at Qingliang Temple in Shanxi Province and is of a primitive style (Fig.16). A number of *xuan-ji* pendants were unearthed together with toothed bronze rings, with trace of patina on surface. Such a pendant should have been used together with the bronze ring (Fig.17-1, 2).

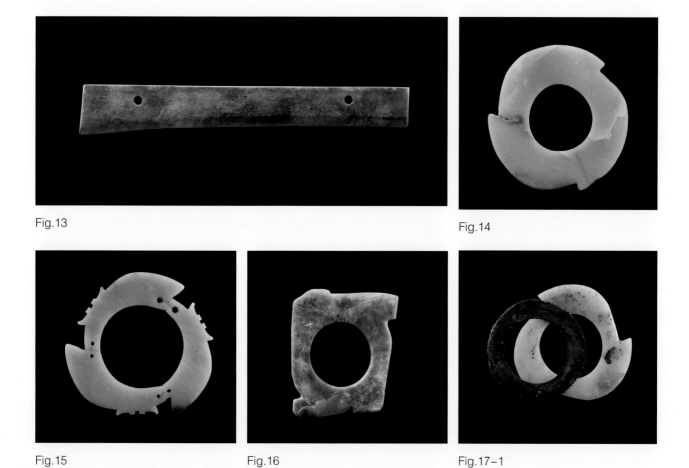

Fig.13

Fig.14

Fig.15

Fig.16

Fig.17-1

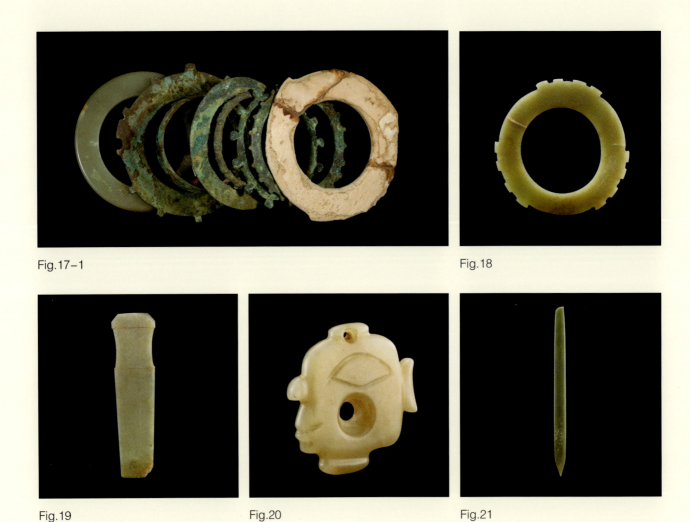

Fig.17−1

Fig.18

Fig.19

Fig.20

Fig.21

There is another type of *xuan-ji*-shaped ring, the outer edge of which is carved with 3-4 groups of protruding edges (Fig.18). It may be the imitation of a toothed bronze ring.

7. Handle-shaped pieces: Such a piece is of a flat bar shape, with a mushroom-shaped top. The end is decorless. There must have been inlaid with a handle-shaped lacquer ware (Fig.19). Handle-shaped pieces were popular in the late Shang Dynasty. The one unearthed in Shimao Site is one of the earliest material objects. It may be something to tell the identity of a clan member, similar to today's identity card.

8. Accessories: This type includes some smaller pierced jade accessories, jade hairpin heads, jade tubes and stringed accessories of various materials. The recognized images of jade accessories include human figures, birds, fish, snakes and cicadas. The most important piece is a human head profile, which features large eyes, the lop ear and the hooked nose. There is a hole in the face. The piece looks extremely like the one collected in Shimao Site in the 1970's (Fig.20).

9. Implements mainly include jade gravers and jade

boring crowns. The handle of a jade graver is thin and long, with one awl-shaped end (Fig.21). Some gravers were remade from the eagle-headed jade hairpins from Shijiahe Culture. On the larger end of a piece there is a nipple-shaped boring crown and the other end remains tenon-shaped as before, to stick the rod in. Some boring crowns are worn out and the patterns are unrecognizable, due to long-time use and friction (Fig.22-1, 2).

II. Textures of Shimao jades vary greatly among different shapes. On the whole, jade axes, battle-axes and knives are made of various materials, including tremolite, actynolin, silexite, griotte marble, and serpentinized griotte marble. Varying in transparency and hardness, jades made of the aforementioned materials are coarse in texture, have impurities, cracks and flaws, and are of various colors, usually grey, cyan, green, brown and black. There are even more than one color in the same jade piece. Bi pendants, rings and *xuan-ji* pendants are made of good jade, generally of tremolite. The material is pure in texture and has a waxy luster. A *xuan-ji* pendant, in particular, is made of fine-textured jade. The color is usually yellowish green, green and bluish white.

Few Shimao jades have impregnation. The jade texture is largely seeable. Some jades are partly impregnated. Soil impregnation is usually grayish white or grayish brown (Fig.23). Iron impregnation is of various brown hues (coffee hues). In a brown-hue impregnation there is usually a sort of grayish yellow impregnation that is often seen in jades from Qijia Culture (Fig.24).

Techniques found in Shimao jades are as follows: 1. Cutting. The technique of cutting raw materials is quite mature. The cut surface is smooth. Slicing is found in most cases; thus, there are often traces of dislocation from bevelment. Occasionally, the trace of linear cutting is detected. A saw is only 1-2mm thick at the thinnest place (Fig.25). It's conjectured that the metal straight saw was already in use at the time (as indicated by the bronze knives and stone moulds unearthed from Shimao Site) and such a saw was quite stable in operation. There may have been simply-constructed lathe-like machines. 2.

Fig.22-1   Fig.22-2   Fig.23

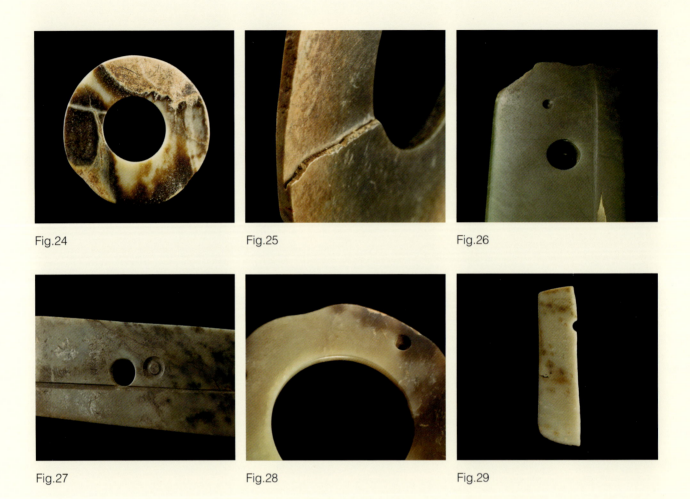

Fig.24　　　　　　　　　Fig.25　　　　　　　　　Fig.26

Fig.27　　　　　　　　　Fig.28　　　　　　　　　Fig.29

Piercing. There are solid and hollow drills. A solid drill was used to pierce smaller holes on axes, battle-axes, knives and *huang*-semicircular pendants. Such a hole was drilled from one side (Fig.26). A hollow drill was used to pierce larger holes on bi pendants, rings, *xuan-ji* pendants, and jade knives. Such a hole was drilled from one side (Fig.27). A hole drilled from one side was flare shaped, wider at the end from which the drill drilled in. It is commonly seen on pieces from late Longshan Culture. But the holes on jade bi pendants, rings and xuan-ji pendants unearthed from Shimao Site were well trimmed. That is, the pointed parts in the hole were ground (commonly known as

daoleng), so as to get the smooth hole wall (Fig.28). 3. Splitting and remaking. Splitting refers to crosscutting a flat jade ware. No polishing is applied on the cut surface. A jade piece may be crosscut into two, four or even eight pieces (Fig.29). In this way, the original shape of a jade piece would be preserved, while the number of pieces was multiplied. Remaking refers to cut and remake a jade piece into another shape. For example, two jade battle-axes were remade from a jade *zhang* tablet. On one of the two battle-axes there are the protruding edge and intaglio lines of the *zhang* tablet (Fig.30-1, 2). There is a jade bracelet that was cut from a jade *cong* with immortal being and animal mask

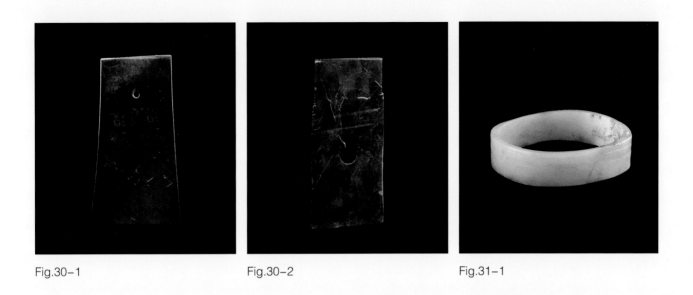

Fig.30-1   Fig.30-2   Fig.31-1

Fig.31-2   Fig.32-1

patterns of Liangzhu Culture. As shown by the pattern left on the bracelet, the *cong* was cut into four bracelets (Fig.31-1, 2). In a word, cropping and cutting techniques were quite developed for Shimao jades. It is noteworthy that traces left by an emery wheel are detected on some jades; that is, the cutting trace is shuttle shaped. On both ends of such a trace there are dense and fine radial lines (commonly known as *paodao or chudao*) (Fig.32-1, 2).

III. Reflections

It has taken us quite a long time to see the significance of Shimao jades. Jade ware unearthed from Shimao Site was first got known by people in the late Qing Dynasty. Wu Dacheng was Education Administrator of Shaanxi-Gansu Region based in Xi'an between 1872 and 1876, during which period he collected jades largely from Northern Shaanxi, including jade knives, zhang tablets, bi pendants, rings, and xuan-ji pendants. Twenty-eight jade

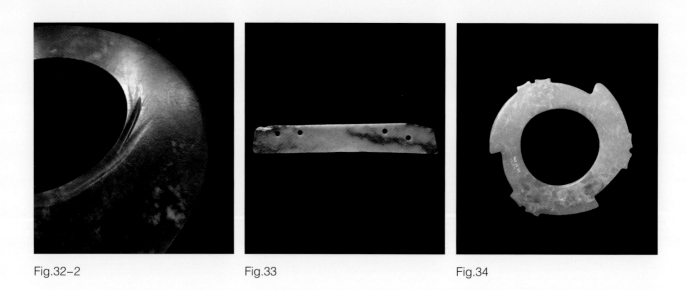

Fig.32-2   Fig.33   Fig.34

pieces from Wu's collection are now in the collection of the Royal Ontario Museum, Canada. The jade knife (No. 928.12.81, Fig.33) and xuan-ji pendant (No. 928.12.57, Fig.34) are extremely similar to those collected in this catalogue [2]. The period of the Republic of China (1911-1949) saw a peak of outflow of Chinese cultural relics, including Shimao-unearthed jades that flew in large numbers into academic institutes and museums in Europe and Americas. The U.S. sees the largest inflow of Shimao jades [3]. Shimao jades played a significant role in the early study of jades. Shimao jades are mostly large in size and of geometric shapes, similar to the ritual vessels described in ancient documents. Thus, Wu Dacheng held that Shimao jades were made for ritual purpose during the Xia, Shang and Zhou dynasties. He made close textural research on the naming and usage of Shimao jades, in accordance with Confucian classics such as *Zhouli* (*Rites of Zhou*). Wu published his research results in *Guyu Tukao* (*Catalogue of Ancient Jades*) completed in 1889 [4]. In the United States, Berthold Laufer, who was the Western

pioneer in the study of Chinese jades, thought highly of Wu Dacheng's textual research. In his *Jade: A Study in Chinese Archaeology and Religion* published in 1912, Laufer quoted almost all of Wu's descriptions of jade ritual vessels [5]. It is interesting that Laufer claimed in his book that there was neither a prehistoric era nor a Neolithic Age or era of stoneware making or using in China. But it's not surprising to find such a ridiculous statement back in the time when archaeology wasn't even introduced to China. It was thanks to Laufer's effort that ancient Chinese jades were collected and pursued in the West in the early 20th century. Laufer not only energetically introduced ancient Chinese jades to the Western audience in an academic way, he was also zealous of Chinese jade ware [6]. Under his influence, renowned collectors in the U.S., such as Charles Lang Freer, Edward Sonnenschein, Grenvill L. Winthrop, Alfred F. Pillsbury, Chauncy Hamlin, Wyman Drummond and Arthur M. Sackler, collected Shimao jades, and those collected items took an important position in exhibitions. Also, it was thanks to the popularity of Laufer's work in

Europe and the U.S. that Wu Dacheng and his *Guyu Tukao* (*Catalogue of Ancient Jades*) became known to foreigners. And collectors outside China scrambled for "Wu Dacheng's Jades" and were all eager to have a look [7].

The passed-down Shimao jades found by the 1970's had been largely toothed *zhang* tablets, axes, battle-axes and knives, as they were found when local farmers dug the city walls or in occasionally-seen sacrificial pits when local farmers leveling the ground (Fig.35-1, The pit is at the point of the arrow; Fig.35-2, The east gate site was seen from the pit.) But the specific localities of excavation had remained unknown, until 1976 when Dai Yingxin made a field survey at Shimao Site and collected over 100 pieces of jade ware, making a preliminary recognition of the localities of excavation and times of the jades and unveiling the mystery of Shimiao jades [8]. Jade bi pendants, rings and *xuan-ji* pendants unearthed in large numbers from pit tombs at Shimao Site have come known to people since the 1990s. According to rough statistics, there are 3,000-4,000 pieces of Shimao jade ware in the collection of domestic and foreign cultural and archaeological institutions and in private collections at home and abroad [9].

As shown by presently-available data, Shimao jades have been largely unearthed from the stone-lined city walls or house foundations, sacrificial pits (or cellars) and large-scale pit tombs. The jades unearthed

Fig.35-1

Fig.35-2

from the stone-lined city walls or house foundations are mainly original wares or dissected axes, battle-axes, knives and *zhang* tablets. The ones unearthed from sacrificial pits are mostly *zhang* tablets, battle-axes and knives. The pieces unearthed from pit tombs are largely jade rings and *xuan-ji* pendants.

Quite a number of jades were unearthed from the jade pits at Xinhua Site 1996-1999 and from Shimao Site since 2011. Both sites are in the Shenmu County, Shaanxi Province. Those jades have provided solid data to accurately date Shimao jades. Xinhua Site is about 20km away from Shimao Site and the two sites were from the same culture. From the jade pit (K1) at Xinhua Site were unearthed 36 jades, including battle-axes, spades, knives, axes, rings, *huang*-semicircular pendants and *zhang* tablets. At discovery, they were found to be vertically inserted into earth in six lines and parallel to each other. Xinhua Site is estimated between 2150-1900BC and to overlap with the Xia calendar [10]. In the excavation of the east city gate of Shimao Site, 21 jades were unearthed, including

Fig.36

spades, *zhang* tablets, *huang*-semicircular pendants, knives and adzes. The localities of discovery were largely clearly marked, serving as the key data of the burial of Shimao jades [11].

Shimao Site is estimated between late Longshan Culture (2300-2200BC) and early Xia Dynasty (2000-1900BC) [12]. In actuality, Shimao jades we see today are mostly of early Xia Dynasty. Then what do the ones from late Longshan Culture look like? What differences are there between those from late Longshan Culture and those of early Xia Dynasty? It may require more and further archaeological excavations and data.

What are feature objects of Shimao jades? It is hard to answer, in fact. For most of Shimao jades were found from other earlier or contemporaneous cultures; for example, jade *bi* pendants, rings, toothed *zhang* tablets, axes, battle-axes, knives and *cong* were commonly found in jade objects from Qijia Culture and Taosi Culture. *Xuan-ji* pendants and toothed *zhang* tablets may two representative types of Shimao jades. *Xuan-ji* pendants unearthed from Shimao Site are known for their jade quality, large number and various shapes. This is unrivalled by the other contemporaneous cultures. What's more important, *xuan-ji* pendants were unearthed together with toothed bronze rings. The pendant and bronze ring formed a set, which was used for a certain religious purpose. They are of great significance in understanding and knowing more about the spiritual world of the ancient residents in Shimao City. We'll say no more about toothed *zhang* tablets here, as the type is one of the hottest academic topics and there are innumerable research and arguments about it. The aforementioned two types of jades must have originated from Shimao and been introduced to the Central Plains and southeastern China. Shimao jades indicate frequent intertribal material exchanges back at the time. For instance, there are jade bi pendants, *cong* and knives similar to those from Qijia Culture or Taosi Culture, or jade *cong* similar to those from Liangzhu Culture, jade cicadas similar to those from Hongshan Culture, as well as deep-carved jade accessories (Fig.36) and eagle-shaped hairpin heads similar to those from Shijiahe Culture. The jade ware style represented by jades from Shimao and Xinhua sites in the Shenmu County is found in northern Shaanxi and neighboring southern Inner Mongolia, known as "the jade style of Hetao Area" [13]. The author used to hold that the area of Shimao Site bordered Qijia Culture in the west and Taosi Culture in the east, and those areas together formed a vast region of jade culture. Also, it fell on the formative stage of the Road of Jade. Thus, Shimao serves as a solid evidence of the origin and development of Road of Jade [14].

Fig.37-1

Fig.37-2

The last question: Where did the jade-loving ancient resident in Shimao go? It's an interesting question to be pondered over. Shimao City was not an isolated one in its times. There were nearly 100 stone-walled settlements, varying in size, along the Yellow River at the place where Shaanxi and Shanxi joined. Those "satellite villages or secondary centers" around Shimao Site were like stars around the moon and in 400-500 years they served as the solid social foundation for "the royal state Shimao". Finally, an early state represented by Shimao Site emerged [15]. It's quite interesting that the stone-walled settlements, Shimao City itself included, were abandoned at almost the same time. As what's been found in the east city gate and the royal complex platform of Shimao Site indicates, the architectures inside the city were not damaged by war and there was no trace of burning or collapsing (Fig.37-1, 2). The residents voluntarily abandoned the site in a peaceful manner and left in a good order. The large jades that have been discovered may have nothing to do with sacrificial purposes. Instead, the residents buried the large jades which they were unable to be carry with them when leaving the city. It is particularly evident in the jade pit (K1) in Xinhua Site. The pit is rectangular shaped in plan. The two shorter sides are convex, while the two long sides are slightly concave into a wasp-waisted shape. The pit measures 1.40m long, 0.45-0.50m wide and 0.12-0.22m deep. The walls are coarse without further finishing. Some places have collapsed or damaged. The bottom is flat and smooth. The entire pit seems to be made in a hurry [16].

Then why the ancient residents of Shimao City left such a grand site with their sacred jades? Because the Xia Dynasty was established in the Central Plains. The archaeological excavation conducted in Yuhui Village, Bengbu, Anhui Province, was the first piece of evidence for the authenticity of the ancient legend that "Yu met vassals at Tushan" [17]. The event first of all changed the crown abdication into hereditary system for leadership of tribal union. Qi, who was Yu's son, established the Xia Dynasty. Secondly, the tribal merger that had lasted for two or three centuries from late Longshan Culture onwards came to an end and the major tribes submitted themselves to the rule of Yu. Yu later divided the land under his rule in nine administrative regions. One of the most effective ruling ways was to relocate people from their hometowns to other places and put them under the centralized administration. It can be conjectured here that from the rule of Yu the Great to Qi of Xia and his successors, the rulers relocated tribal people from their hometowns to other places under the centralized administration. Shimao City was no exception. As for the development of jades, jade objects like toothed zhang tablets and knives were gradually replaced by jade dagger-axes and handle-shaped pieces that symbolized status and identity. It is likely to remain unknown forever where the ancient people of Shimao City were relocated. There are some toothed zhang tablets and jade knives in the relics from Erlitou Culture of the Xia Dynasty in Henan Province [18]. They are the last survivor of Shimao jades in the Xia Dynasty in the Central Plains. Toothed zhang tablets seemed to be of a strong vitality. They disappeared in the Central Plains and were introduced to southwest and southeast China. The process didn't end until the Western Zhou Dynasty. We may see the route of toothed zhang tablets as the migration route of the ancient people of Shimao City and their descendants.

Notes

[1] Wang Weilin and Sun Zhouyong, "Time of Shimao Jades and Related Questions", in Archaeology and Cultural Relics, 2011 (4). Sun Zhouyong and Shao Jing, "On the Background of the Excavation of Shimao Jades", in Spirit of Jade: Anthology of the Symposium on Ancient Chinese Jades and Traditional Chinese Culture (VI), Hangzhou: Zhejiang Ancient Books Publishing House, 2014.

[2] Shen Chen and Gu Fang, Ancient Chinese Jades from the Royal Ontario Museum, Beijing: Cultural Relics Press, 2016, Fig.012, Fig.023.

[3] Jiang Yili, Gu Fang, Early Chinese Jade In American Museums, Beijing: Science Press, 2009.

[4] Wu Dacheng, Guyu Tukao (Catalogue of Ancient Jades), block-printed edition, Shanghai: Tongwen Bookstore, 1889.

[5] Berthold Laufer, Jade: A Study in Chinese Archaeology and Religion, Chicago: Field Museum of Natural History, 1912.

[6] Jiang Yili, "Collectors of Ancient Chinese Jades in the Early 20th Century U.S.", in Jiang Yili and Gu Fang, Early Chinese Jade In American Museums, Beijing: Science Press, 2009.

[7] Shen Chen, "Being Together and Apart: Wu Dacheng and His Collection of Jades" , SuZhou Museum, Collections of the Wu Family from Suhou in the Qing Dynasty, Yilin Press, 2017.

[8] Dai Yingxin, "A Field Survey of Shimao Site from Longshan Culture in Shenmu County, Shaanxi Province", in Archaeology, 1977 (2); "Shimao Jades from Longshan Culture in Shenmu County", in Archaeology and Cultural Relics, Issue 5 and 6, 1988; "Discovery of Shimao Jades from Longshan Culture in Shenmu County, I-VI", in The National Palace Museum Monthly of Chinese Art, Issue 125-130, 1998 (8)-(12), 1994 (1).

[9] Sun Zhouyong and Shao Jing, "On the Background of the Excavation of Shimao Jades", in Spirit of Jade: Anthology of the Symposium on Ancient Chinese Jades and Traditional Chinese Culture (VI), Hangzhou: Zhejiang Ancient Books Publishing House, 2014.

[10] Shaanxi Provincial Institute of Archaeology and Yulin Municipal Institute of Cultural Relics, Xinhua Site in Shenmu County, Beijing: Science Press, 2005. Sun Zhouyong, "On Jades Unearthed from Xinhua Site in Shenmu County", in Zhongyuan Wenwu (Cultural Relics of Central China), 2002 (5).

[11] Sun Zhouyong and Shao Jing, "On the Background of the Excavation of Shimao Jades", in Spirit of Jade: Anthology of the Symposium on Ancient Chinese Jades and Traditional Chinese Culture (VI), Hangzhou: Zhejiang Ancient Books Publishing House, 2014.

[12] Sun Zhouyong and Shao Jing, "On the Background of the Excavation of Shimao Jades", in Spirit of Jade: Anthology of the Symposium on Ancient Chinese Jades and Traditional Chinese Culture (VI), Hangzhou: Zhejiang Ancient Books Publishing House, 2014.

[13] Wang Weilin and Sun Zhouyong, "Time of Shimao Jades and Related Questions", in Archaeology and Cultural Relics, 2011 (4).

[14] Gu Fang, "Ideas on the Time of Formation and Routes of the Road of Jade", in Archaeology and Cultural Relics, 2004 supplement.

[15] Sun Zhouyong and Shao Jing, "Shimao: Past, Present and Future", in Shaanxi Provincial Institute of Archaeology, Yulin Municipal Archaeological Exploration Team, Shenmu County Cultural Artifact Bureau, and Shimao Site Administration of Shenmu County, Discovery of the Shimao Archaic City, Beijing: Cultural Relics Press, 2016.

[16] Shaanxi Provincial Institute of Archaeology and Yulin Municipal Institute of Cultural Relics, Xinhua Site in Shenmu County, Beijing: Science Press, 2005.

[17] The Institute of Archaeology CASS and Bengbu Museum of Anhui Province, Yuhui Village in Bengbu, Beijing: Science Press, 2013.

[18] The Institute of Archaeology CASS, Erlitou Site in Yanshi, Beijing: Encyclopedia of China Publishing House, 1999.

001 玉 璧

直径 16.2 厘米　内径 6.9 厘米　厚 0.7 厘米

青白玉质，温润细腻。扁平圆形，素面无纹，表面受沁呈土黄
色和深褐色。内壁打磨光滑，外缘较不规则，有人工切割痕迹。

002 玉　璧

直径 16.2 厘米　内径 5.15~5.35 厘米
厚 0.15~0.3 厘米

白玉质，温润透亮。扁平圆形，表
面光素无纹，局部裂绺处受沁呈黄
褐色。内壁圆滑，单面钻，外缘规
整，极薄，有人工切痕，稍有残缺。
为分剖改制器。

003 玉 璧

直径 12.25~12.3 厘米　内径 6.48~6.9 厘米　厚 0.3~0.65 厘米

青玉质，温润细腻。扁平圆形，表面光素无纹，局部裂绺
处受沁严重呈黄褐色和黑色。外缘较不规则，孔壁圆滑，
边缘较薄，有人工切割痕迹。

004 玉 璧

直径 8.8~9.1 厘米　内径 3.6 厘米　厚 0.45 厘米

青白玉质，温润细腻。扁平圆形，表面光素无纹，局部裂
绺处受沁呈灰白褐色和黑色。外缘较不规则，孔壁圆滑，
边缘较薄。

005 玉 璧

直径 14.95~15.1 厘米　内径 5.7~6 厘米　厚 0.55~0.7 厘米

青玉质，杂质较多。扁平圆形，表面光素无纹，局部
裂络处受沁呈深褐色和黑色。外缘打磨较不规整，孔
壁圆滑，边缘较薄。

006 玉 璧

直径 13.5 厘米　内径 6.83~7.2 厘米　厚 0.2~0.42 厘米
青玉质，较为温润，略有杂质。扁平圆形，表面光素
无纹，器表受沁呈灰褐色。外缘内壁较为圆滑规整，
稍有残缺。

007 玉 璧

直径 13.79~13.9 厘米　内径 6.39~6.5 厘米　厚 0.05~0.25 厘米

青玉质，温润透亮。扁平圆形，表面光素无纹，局部绺裂处
受沁呈黄褐色，绺裂处如冰裂纹。外缘内壁圆滑规整，有人
工切痕，稍有残缺，为分剖改制。

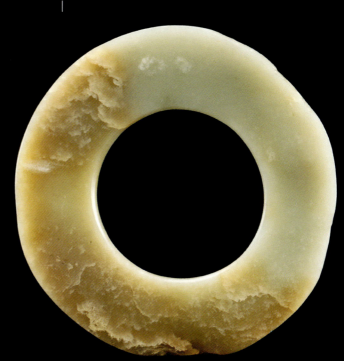

008 玉 璧

直径 12.55~12.89 厘米　内径 6.4~6.5 厘米
厚 0.25~0.45 厘米

青白玉质，温润透亮。扁平圆形，表面光素无纹，
局部裂绺处受沁呈黄褐色。内壁圆滑规整，外缘
不规则，有人工切痕。

009 玉 璧

直径 14.1~14.2 厘米　内径 5.85 厘米
厚 0.2~0.65 厘米

青玉质，表面光素无纹。扁平圆形，
外缘内壁圆滑规整，局部受沁呈
灰褐色。内壁留有管钻的痕迹，
为单面钻孔，是齐家玉器工艺的
典型特点。器表留有极薄的锯缝，
呈 V 字形。

010 玉　璧

直径 12.8 厘米　内径 6.2 厘米　厚 0.6 厘米

青玉质，温润细腻。扁平圆形，表面光素无纹，
局部受沁呈灰褐色和褐色。外缘内壁打磨规整，
孔壁圆滑，有砣具碾琢痕迹。

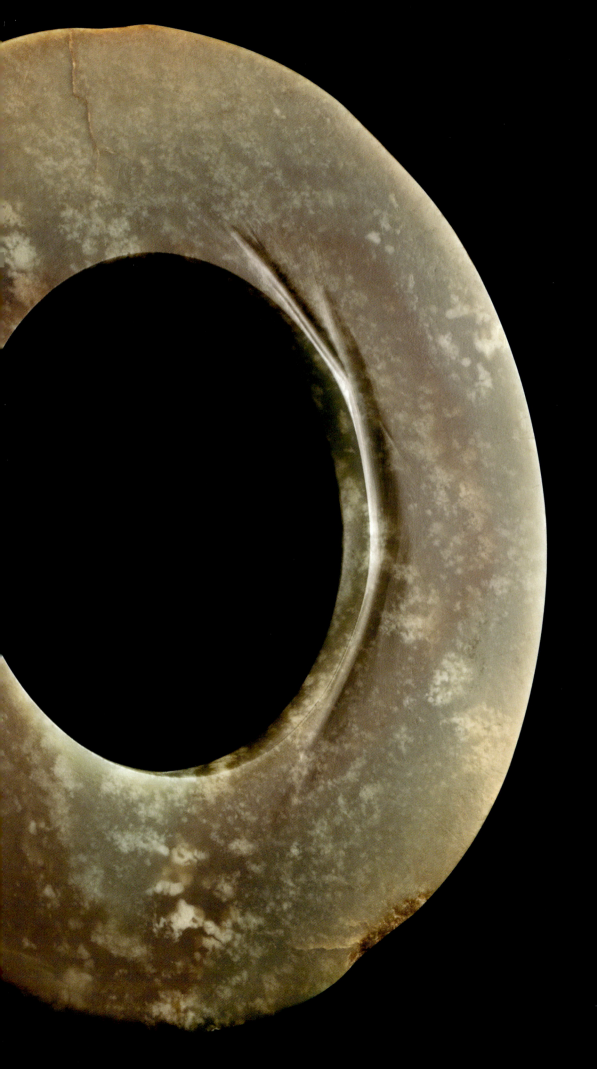

011 玉 璧

直径 14.8~15.3 厘米　内径 7.4~7.6 厘米
厚 0.1~0.2 厘米

青玉质，带黑点条纹，温润透亮。墨
点与白色玉质交相辉映，形成水墨画
般的艺术美感，极富韵律。此璧是将
一件完整的玉璧一剖为二而成的改制
作品，剖面留有切割台痕，薄如蝉翼，
是石峁玉器的典型特征，也反映了石
峁玉工高超的加工水平。

012 玉 璧

直径 12.69~12.79 厘米　内径 6.35~6.55 厘米
厚 0.3~0.45 厘米

青玉质，较为温润。扁平圆形，素面无纹，
表面受沁呈黄褐色。外缘内壁圆滑规整，
内壁为单面钻孔，具有齐家文化玉器风格。

013 玉　璧

直径 13.7~14.2 厘米　内径 6.55~6.61 厘米　厚 0.15~0.35 厘米

青白玉质，较为温润。扁平圆形，玉璧表面光素无纹，局
部裂绺处受沁呈褐色。孔壁打磨圆滑规整，外缘较为规则，
有残断。

014 玉 璧

直径 12.62~12.65 厘米　内径 6.54~6.68 厘米　厚 0.38 厘米

青白玉质，较为温润。扁平圆形，表面光素无纹，局部裂
绺受沁呈褐色和黑色。外缘内壁很规整，打磨圆滑规整，
有人工切痕。

015 玉 璧

直径 14.8 厘米　内径 6.64~6.8 厘米　厚 0.19~0.48 厘米

白玉质，黑色带状纹理，温润细腻。扁平圆形，素面
无纹，有人工切痕。外缘内壁圆滑规整，有残断。

016 玉 璧

直径 9.48~10.2 厘米　内径 2.9~2.93 厘米　厚 0.65~1.02 厘米

青玉质。不规则扁平圆形，素面无纹，表面受沁呈土褐色。内壁打磨圆滑规整，孔壁为单面钻孔，留有管钻痕迹，为齐家玉器工艺的典型特点，外缘较不规则。器表留有片切割的痕迹。

017 玉　璧

直径 12.6~12.8 厘米　内径 6.2 厘米　厚 0.8 厘米

青玉质，温润细腻。扁平圆形，素面无纹，表面受沁
呈灰白色和浅褐色。内壁打磨光滑，外缘较不规则，
璧两面做稍加打洼处理。

018 玉　璧

直径 12.2~13.1 厘米　内径 6.6~7.4 厘米　厚 0.75 厘米

青白玉质，温润细腻。不规则扁平圆形，表面光素无纹，
局部裂绺处受沁呈黄褐色。外缘打磨较不规整，孔壁圆滑，
有切割痕迹。

019 玉 璧

直径 15.5~16.2 厘米　内径 6.5 厘米　厚 0.3~0.4 厘米
青玉质，温润细腻。扁平圆形，素面无纹，表面
绺裂处受沁呈土黄色和深褐色。内壁打磨光滑，
外缘较为规整，有人工切割痕迹。

020 玉 璧

外径 12.4　内径 6.5 厘米　厚 0.5 厘米

青玉质，温润细腻。扁平圆形，素面无纹，表面受沁呈灰白
色和深褐色。内壁外缘打磨光滑，一侧有一斜形切口。另一
侧有两个钻孔。这种做法的玉璧，在石峁玉器中属首例，对
其功能和用途有待进一步探讨。

021 玉 璧

直径 15.3~15.5 厘米　内径 7.12~7.18 厘米
厚 0.2~0.52 厘米

青玉质，温润细腻。扁平圆形，素面无纹，表
面绺裂处受沁呈灰白色、土黄色和深褐色。内
壁打磨光滑，外缘较为规整，有人工切割痕迹。

022 玉 璧

直径 13.78~13.99 厘米　内径 7.47~7.5 厘米
厚 0.2~0.4 厘米

青黄玉质，温润细腻。扁平圆形，素面无纹，
表面绺裂处受沁呈灰白色和深褐色。内壁打
磨光滑，外缘较为规整。

023 玉 璧

直径 11.39~11.6 厘米　内径 6.55~6.6 厘米
厚 0.52~0.6 厘米

青玉质,温润细腻。扁平圆形,素面无纹,表面绺裂
处有受沁呈灰白色和深褐色。内壁打磨光滑,外缘较
为规整。

024 玉 璧

直径 13.35~13.41 厘米　内径 6.67~6.72 厘米
厚 0.3 厘米

青黄玉质，温润细腻。扁平圆形，素面无纹，
表面绺裂处受沁呈灰白色和深褐色。内壁打磨
光滑，外缘不规整。

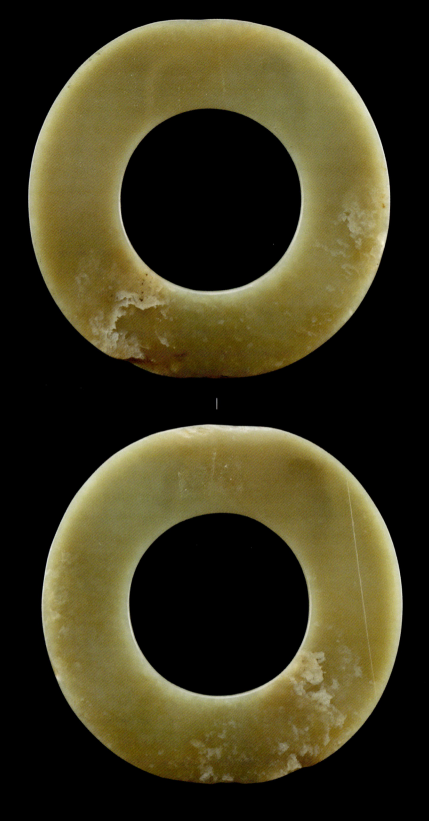

025 玉　璧

直径 12.6~13.7 厘米　内径 6.8~7.1 厘米　厚 0.5~0.52 厘米

青黄玉质，温润细腻。扁平圆形，素面无纹，表面绺裂处受沁呈灰白
色和褐色。内壁打磨光滑，外缘较为规整，有人工切割痕迹。

026 玉　璧

直径 13.16~13.29　内径 6.6~6.7 厘米　厚 0.65~0.83 厘米

青黄玉质，温润细腻。扁平圆形，素面无纹，表面绺裂处
受沁呈灰白色和深褐色。内壁打磨光滑，外缘较为规整。

027 玉 璧

直径 11.05~11.2 厘米　内径 5.45~6.0 厘米
厚 0.7~0.78 厘米

青玉质，温润细腻。扁平圆形，素面无纹，
表面绺裂处受沁呈灰白色和灰褐色。内壁打
磨光滑，外缘较为规整。

028 玉　璧

直径 9.93~10.2 厘米　内径 4.51~4.75 厘米
厚 0.5~0.65 厘米

青玉质，温润细腻。扁平圆形，素面无纹，表面
绺裂处受沁呈灰白色和深褐色。内壁打磨光滑，
外缘较为规整。

直径 8.12~8.3 厘米　内径 4.29~4.55 厘米　厚 0.35~0.68 厘米

青黄玉质，温润细腻。扁平圆形，素面无纹，表面绺裂处受
沁呈灰白色和深褐色。内壁打磨光滑，外缘较为规整，有人
工切割痕迹。

030 玉 璧

直径 12.55 厘米　厚 0.65 厘米　高 1.3 厘米

内径 6.52~7.4 厘米　孔沿宽 0.3~0.35 厘米

青玉质，温润细腻。内孔边缘两面凸起，亦称"有领玉璧"或"突缘玉璧"。局部裂绺处受沁呈灰黄褐色和黑色。外缘内壁打磨规整，孔壁圆滑，边缘较薄。

二　联璜璧、环

031 联璜璧

直径 11.9~12.2 厘米　内径 5.4~5.5 厘米　厚 0.3~0.39 厘米
青玉质，温润细腻。扁平弧形，呈扇面形，局部受沁
呈黄褐色、黑褐色、灰白色，外缘内壁打磨较为规整
光滑。此三联璧由三件璜组合而成，三璜两端各有孔
相对，可穿线连接起来。

032 联璜璧

直径 11.76~11.88 厘米　内径 6.2~6.23 厘米
厚 0.4~0.6 厘米

白玉质，润泽细腻。扁平圆形，光素无纹，
局部裂绺处受沁呈黄褐色，有黑色斑点，
中孔和外壁打磨光滑，且较为规则。此双
联璧由两件璜组合而成，二璜两端各有孔
相对，可穿线连接起来。

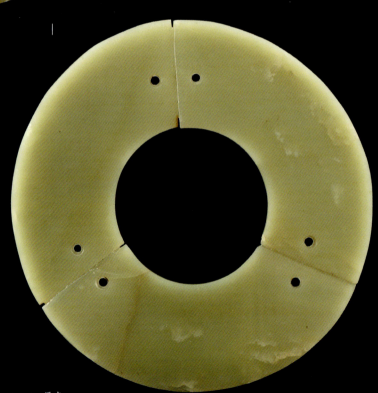

033 联璜璧

直径 12.71~12.8厘米　内径 5.32~5.4厘米　厚 0.12~0.35厘米

青玉质，润泽细腻。扁平圆形，表面光素无纹，局部裂绺处受沁
呈黄褐色和灰白色，中孔和外壁打磨光滑，且较为规则。此三联
璧由三件璜组合而成，三璜两端各有孔相对，可穿线连接起来。
器表有人工切割痕迹。

034 联璜璧

直径 10.83~10.88 厘米　内径 5.73~5.75 厘米
厚 0.12~0.32 厘米

青玉质，细腻润泽。扁平圆形，表面光素无
纹，局部受沁呈灰白色，有黑色斑点，中孔
和外壁打磨较为光滑，且较为规整。此三联
璧由三件璜组合而成，三璜两端各有孔相对，
可穿线连接起来。

035 联璜环

直径 9.18 厘米   内径 5.8 厘米   厚 0.3~0.42 厘米

白玉质，温润细腻，透亮有光泽。扁平圆形，素面无纹，局部受沁呈黄色。孔壁外缘打磨较为光滑规整，此双联璧由两件璜组合而成，二璜两端各有孔相对，一端一孔，另一端两孔，可穿线连接起来。外缘有单面钻孔痕迹，其中一璜上有喇叭状的单面斜孔，上有绿松石圆片镶痕迹。

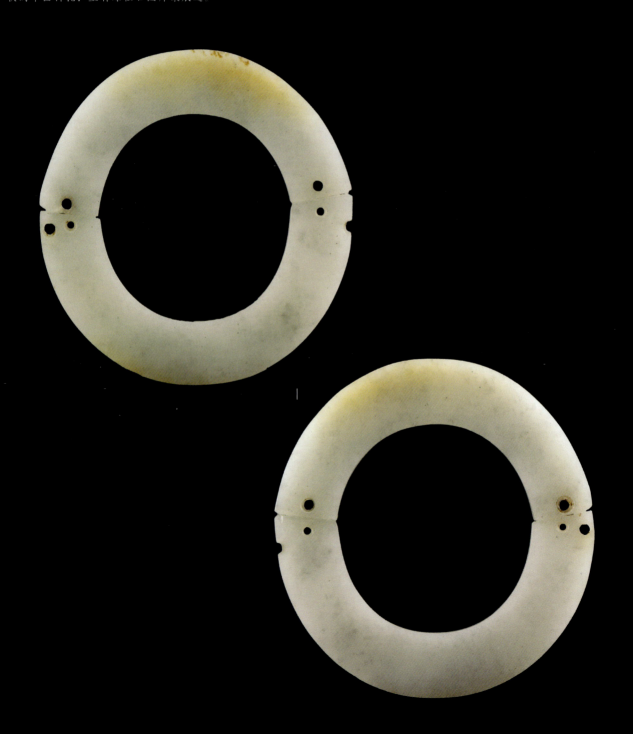

036 联璜环

直径 10.45~11.2 厘米　内径 6~6.35 厘米　厚 0.4~0.55 厘米

白玉质，温润细腻。扁平圆形，表面光素无纹，局部受沁呈黄色和深褐色，孔壁圆滑。此双联璧由两件璜组合而成，二璜两端各有孔相对，可穿线连接起来。

037 联璜环

直径 11.8~12.3 厘米　内径 6.5~6.9 厘米　厚 0.3~0.5 厘米

青黄玉质，温润有光泽。扁平圆形，表面光素无纹，局部裂络处受沁呈褐色。中孔和外壁打磨光滑不规则，表面有弧形线切割痕迹。此双联璧由两件不均等的璜组合而成，二璜两端各有孔相对，可穿连接起来，有穿连使用痕迹，璜一端作平口，一端为斜口。

038 联璜环

直径 9.2～9.6 厘米　内径 5.8～6.3 厘米　厚 0.36～0.5 厘米

白玉质，透润有光泽。扁平圆形，素面无纹，局部受
沁呈黄褐色。此双联璧由两件璜组合而成，二璜两端
各有孔相对，呈喇叭状的单面斜孔，可穿线连接起来。
一璜有破裂，再穿孔将破裂处连接。

039 联璜环

直径 10.1~10.6 厘米　内径 6 厘米　厚 0.2~0.59 厘米

青白玉质，温润细腻。扁平圆形，表面朴素无纹，局部受沁呈褐色和灰白色。外缘打磨不是很规整。此三联璧由三件璜组合而成，三璜两端各有孔相对，可穿线连接起来。

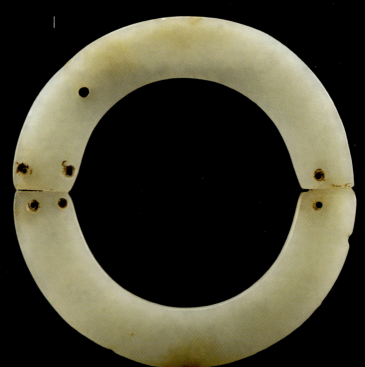

040 联璜环

直径 9.18 厘米　内径 5.8 厘米　厚 0.3~0.42 厘米

白玉质，温润细腻，透亮有光泽。扁平圆形，素面无纹，局部受
沁呈黄色，孔壁外缘打磨较为光滑规整。此双联璧由两件璜组合
而成，二璜两端各有孔相对，一端一孔，另一端两孔，可穿线连
接起来。外缘有单面钻孔痕迹，其中一璜上有喇叭状的单面斜孔，
上有绿松石圆片镶嵌。

041 联璜环

直径 10.71~10.89 厘米　内径 6.5~6.7 厘米
厚 0.4~0.52 厘米

青白玉质，润泽细腻。扁平圆形，表面光素
无纹，局部裂绺处受沁呈黄褐色，有黑色斑点。
中孔和外壁打磨光滑，且较为规则。此双联
璧由两件璜组合而成，双璜两端各有孔相对，
可穿线连接起来，有穿连痕迹。

042 联璜环

直径 9.72~9.78 厘米　内径 6.32~6.38 厘米
厚 0.45~0.65 厘米

青白玉质，较为温润，有絮状杂质。扁平
圆形，素面无纹，局部受沁呈黄褐色，中
孔和外壁打磨光滑，呈很规整的圆形。此
双联璧由两件璜组合而成，二璜两端各有
孔相对，可穿线连接起来。

043 联璜环

直径 7.55~7.64 厘米孔　内径 4.2 厘米
厚 0.45 厘米

青玉质，润泽细腻。扁平圆形，表
面光素无纹，局部裂绺处受沁呈黄
褐色，有黑色斑点，中孔和外壁打
磨光滑，外缘不很规则。此双联璧
由两件璜组合而成，二璜两端各有
孔相对，可穿线连接起来。一璜有
残断。

044 联璜环

直径 10.8 厘米　内径 6.4 厘米　厚 0.5 厘米

青白玉质，细腻润泽。扁平圆形，表面光
素无纹，局部裂绺处受沁呈褐色和灰白色，
中孔和外壁打磨光滑，外缘较为规整。此
双联璧由两件不规等的璜组合而成，二璜
两端各有孔相对，可穿线连接起来，璜两
端各有一小单面钻孔。

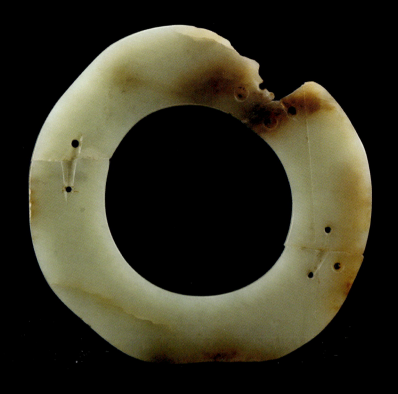

045 联璜环

直径 9.83~10.5 厘米　内径 5.3~5.8 厘米　厚 0.32~0.5 厘米
青白玉质，润泽细腻。扁平圆形，表面光素无纹，局部裂
缝处受沁呈黄褐色和灰白色，中孔和外壁打磨光滑，外缘
很不规整。此三联璧由三件不规等的璜组合而成，三璜两
端各有孔相对，可穿线连接起来，有穿连痕迹。一璜有单
面钻孔，有残缺，器表有人工切割痕迹。

046 联璜环

直径 11.7~11.89 厘米　内径 6.68~6.75 厘米
厚 0.29~0.45 厘米

青绿玉质，润泽细腻。扁平圆形，表面光素
无纹，局部裂绺处受沁呈褐色和灰白色，中
孔和外壁打磨光滑，且较为规则。此三联璧
由三件璜组合而成，三璜两端各有孔相对，
可穿线连接起来。器表有人工切割痕迹。

三　玉　环

047 玉　环

直径 10.28~10.31 厘米　内径 6.65~7.5 厘米
厚 0.45 厘米

青白玉质，温润细腻。扁平圆环状，素
面无纹，局部受沁呈灰白色和黄褐色。
整体圆整光洁，内外壁平滑，玉环中心
稍厚，边缘较薄，通体磨光。

048 玉 环

直径 15~15.2 厘米　内径 12.15~12.45 厘米
厚 0.6~0.65 厘米

青玉质，温润细腻。扁平圆环状，表面
光素无纹，局部受沁呈黑色。整体圆整
光洁，内外壁平直，打磨精致。

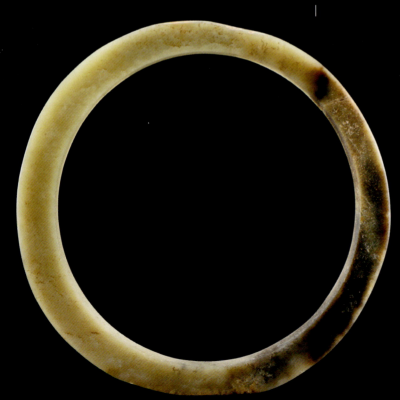

049 玉　环

直径 9.02～9.28 厘米　内径 6.15～6.7 厘米
厚 0.65 厘米

青白玉质，温润细腻，透亮无比。扁平
圆环状，表面光素无纹，局部绺裂处受
沁呈褐色。整体圆整光洁，玉环中心打
磨光滑，边缘较不规则。

050 玉 环

直径 7.6 厘米　内径 5.6 厘米　厚 0.6 厘米

青玉质，扁平圆环状，素面无纹，整体圆整光洁，内外壁平直，局部受沁呈灰白色。中心稍厚，边缘较薄，通体磨光。

051 玉 环

直径 7.2 厘米　内径 5.35 厘米　厚 0.6~0.79 厘米

青灰玉质。扁平圆环状，素面无纹，整体光洁。
内壁平直，外缘光滑，局部有土沁。

052 玉 环

直径 10.8 厘米　内径 7.51 厘米　厚 0.28~0.5 厘米

黄玉质，温润细腻。扁平圆环状，素面无纹，
整体圆整光洁，内外壁平滑，局部受沁呈灰白
色和黄褐色。玉环中心稍厚，边缘较薄，通体
磨光。

053 玉 环

直径 9.78~10.0 厘米　内径 6.4~6.49 厘米　厚 0.54 厘米

青黄玉质，温润细腻。扁平圆环状，素面无纹，局部
受沁呈灰白色。整体圆整光洁，内外壁平滑，玉环中
心稍厚，边缘较薄，通体磨光。

054 玉 环

直径 10.7~10.85 厘米　内径 6.42~6.53 厘米
厚 0.39~0.73 厘米

青黄玉质，温润细腻。扁平圆环状，表
面光素无纹，局部受沁呈褐色和灰白色。
内壁圆整光洁，外缘较不规则，有人工
切割和磨制的痕迹。

055 玉 环

直径 10.9~11.05 厘米　内径 6.55~6.7 厘米
厚 0.55 厘米

青黄玉质，温润透亮，细腻有光泽。扁平
圆环状，素面无纹，局部绺裂处受沁呈褐色。
外缘有不规则磨损，中孔单面钻，有切割
和磨制的痕迹。

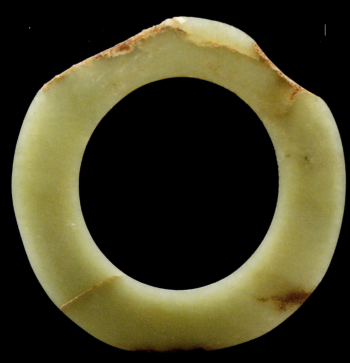

056 玉　环

直径 9.34~9.88 厘米　内径 6.58~6.62 厘米
厚 0.4~0.52 厘米

青黄玉质，温润细腻，透亮有光泽。
扁平圆环状，表面光素无纹，局部受
沁呈深褐色和黑色。整体圆整光洁，
器表有两孔，内壁平滑，外缘有切割
和磨制的豁口。

057 玉 环

直径 8.89~8.97 厘米　内径 5.15~5.2 厘米

厚 0.23~0.49 厘米

黄绿玉质，温润透亮，细腻有光泽。扁平
圆环状，表面光素无纹，局部受沁呈褐色
和灰白色。内壁打磨平滑，外缘有两处人
为磨损。

058 玉　环

直径 9.41~9.72 厘米　内径 6.58~6.6 厘米
厚 0.27~0.4 厘米

青玉质，温润细腻。扁平圆环状，素面
无纹，局部受沁呈黑褐色和灰白色。中
孔单面钻，外缘较不规整，外缘有单面
钻孔，疑为镶嵌绿松石片之用。

为规则，中心稍厚，边缘较薄。

059 玉　环

直径 11.6 厘米　内径 6.7 厘米　厚 0.5 厘米

青黄玉质，较为温润。扁平圆环状，表
面光素无纹，局部裂绺处受沁呈黄褐色
和灰白色。内壁平直光滑，外缘打磨较
为规则，中心稍厚，边缘较薄。

060 玉 环

直径 9.57~9.8 厘米　内径 6.82~7.03 厘米
厚 0.6 厘米

青白玉质，温润细腻。扁平圆环状，素面
无纹，局部受沁呈灰白色和黄褐色。整体
圆整光洁，内外壁平滑，玉环中心稍厚，
边缘较薄，通体磨光。

061 玉 环

直径 8.52 厘米　内径 5.72~6.38 厘米
厚 0.32 厘米　领高 0.79~1.0 厘米

青绿玉质。扁平圆环状，表面光素无纹，局部裂
绺处受沁呈灰白色。内孔边缘两面凸起，亦称"有
领玉环"或"突缘玉环"。外缘内壁打磨规整，
整体圆整光洁，中心稍厚，边缘较薄。

062 玉 环

直径 11.73~12.13 厘米　内径 6.58~6.9 厘米
厚 0.35 厘米

青玉质，有杂质。扁平圆形，表面光素无纹，表面受沁呈灰白色。外缘内壁圆滑规整，外缘边缘较薄呈刀状，抛光较亮，外缘有残缺。

063 镶绿松石玉环

直径 10.19~10.4 厘米　内径 6.08~6.4 厘米

孔径（左）0.5~0.92 厘米　孔径（右）0.55~0.9 厘米

青黄玉质，温润透亮。扁平圆形，局部受沁呈黄褐色、灰色、
褐色。内壁圆滑规整，外缘有一处单面钻半圆形豁口、上方
平行镶嵌二颗绿松石。

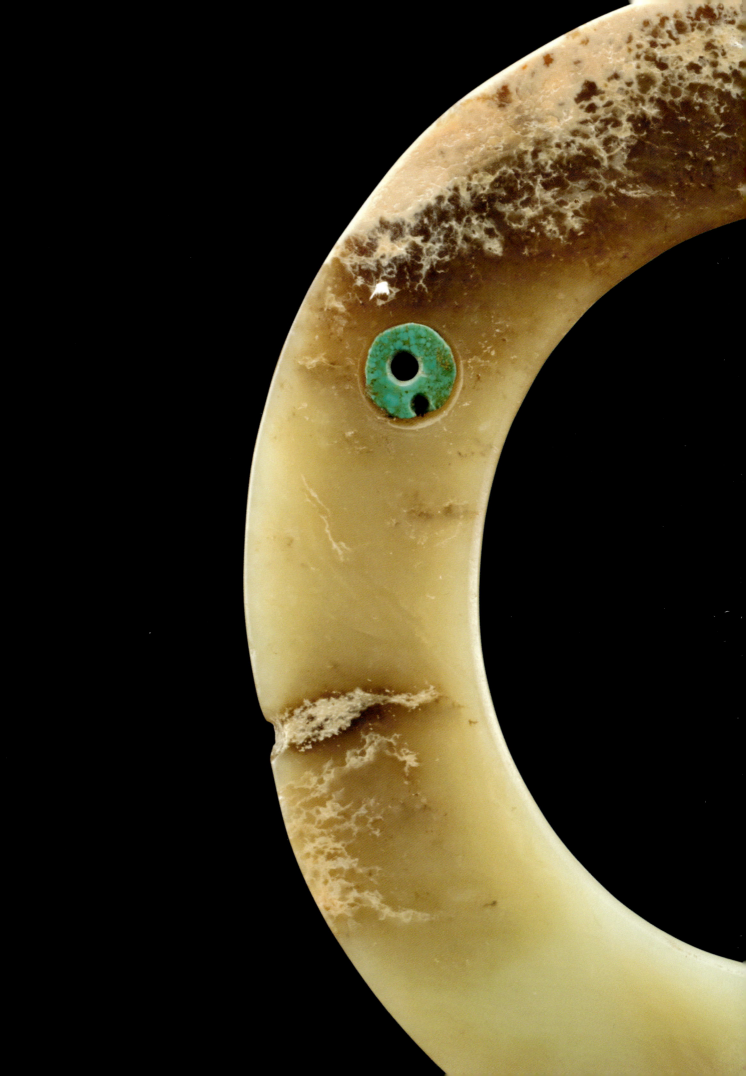

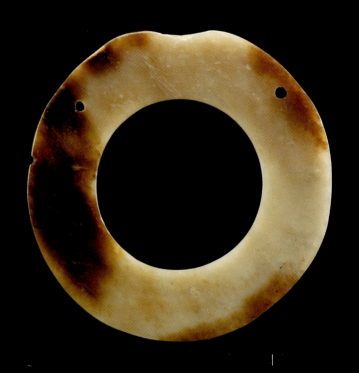

064 玉 环

直径 10.7 厘米　内径 5.7 厘米　厚 0.2~0.5 厘米
白玉质，温润细腻。扁平圆形，局部受沁呈
深褐色和灰白色。孔壁圆滑规整，外缘打磨
不规则，外缘有单面钻孔痕迹，器表有两个
单面钻孔，应为镶嵌绿松石圆片之用，抛光
较亮。

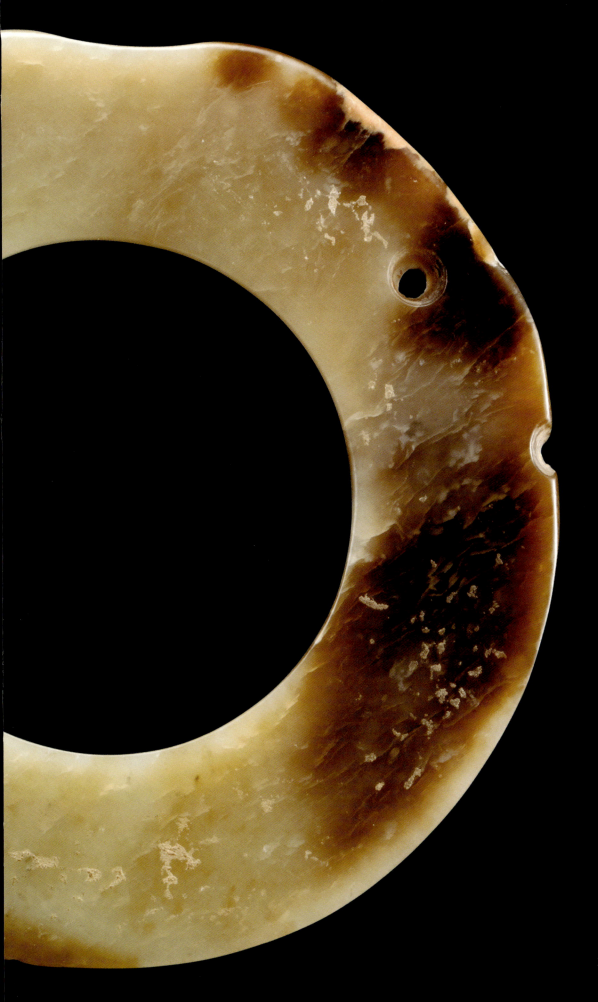

065 玉 环

直径 11.59~11.68 厘米　内径 6~6.66 厘米
厚 0.39~0.5 厘米

青玉质，较为温润。扁平圆形，素面无纹，
表面受沁呈黄褐色和灰白色。外缘内壁
圆滑规整，有残断。

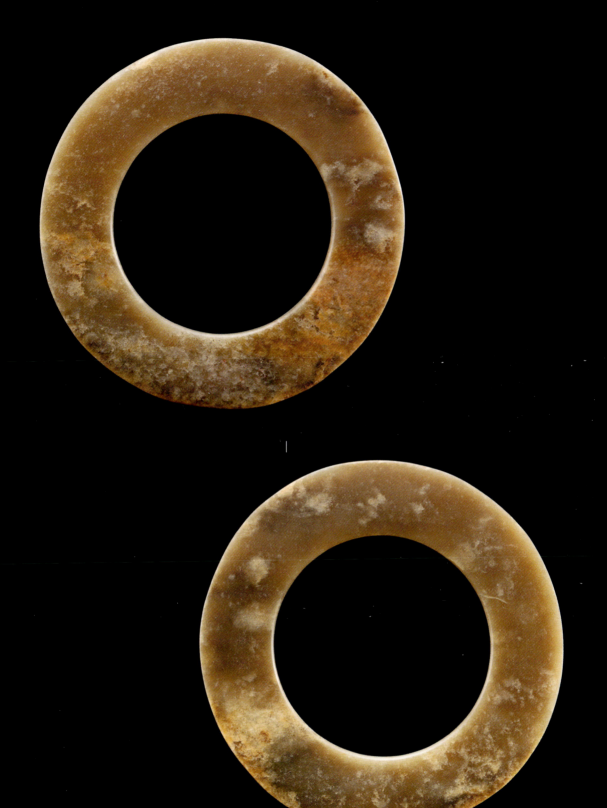

066 玉 环

直径 11.6 厘米　内径 6.9 厘米　厚 0.4 厘米

青黄玉质，温润细腻。扁平圆形，素面无纹，受沁呈黄褐
色和灰白色。外缘内壁打磨圆滑规整，抛光精湛。

067 玉璇玑、玉环、青铜环（一组）

璇玑　直径 11.3　内径 6.5　厚 0.7 厘米
玉环　直径 10.5　内径 6.5　厚 0.7 厘米

璇玑青玉质，呈鸡骨白化，器表遗留有绿色铜锈痕迹。六个布满绿
锈铜环，其中有四个带齿铜环，一个束腰铜镯，这组璇玑、玉环与
带齿铜环同出，应该属于同一组装饰。

玉环青白玉质，温润细腻。扁平圆形，素面无纹，表面留有绿色铜沁。
内壁打磨光滑，外缘较为规整，有人工切割痕迹。

068 玉 环

直径 12.18~12.3 厘米　内径 6.4~6.8 厘米

厚 0.55~0.65 厘米

青玉质，温润细腻。扁平圆形，素面无纹，表面绺
裂处受沁呈灰白色和褐色。内壁打磨光滑，外缘较
为规整。

069 玉　环

直径 11.39~11.6 厘米　内径 6.55~6.6 厘米

厚 0.52~0.6 厘米

青黄玉质。扁平圆形，素面无纹，表面绺裂处受沁呈

灰白色。内壁打磨光滑，外缘较为规整。

070 玉 环

直径 10.48 厘米　内径 6.2 厘米　厚 0.35~1.1 厘米

青玉质。扁平圆形，素面无纹，表面绺裂处受沁呈灰白色
和深褐色。内壁打磨光滑，外缘较为规整。

直径 11.5~11.92 厘米　内径 6.9~8.1 厘米
厚 0.3~0.65 厘米

青玉质，玉质较差，通体受沁严重。扁平圆
形，素面无纹，表面绺裂处受沁呈灰白色和
深褐色。内壁打磨光滑，外缘较为规整，局
部有残。

072 玉 环

直径 12.8~12.9 厘米　内径 6.22~6.28 厘米
厚 0.45~0.6 厘米

青玉质，温润细腻。扁平圆形，玉璧表
面光素无纹，局部受沁呈灰褐色。外缘
较为规则，孔壁打磨圆滑规整，抛光较亮。

四　玉璇玑

073　玉璇玑

直径 13~14.7 厘米　内径 6.9~7.5 厘米
厚 0.1~0.4 厘米

青白玉质，温润细腻，晶莹剔透。体
扁平，局部绺裂处受沁有褐色和灰白
色。由三个带牙玉璜组成，玉璜两端
各有两孔，外缘有三个形状相同、且
均向同一方向旋转的锯齿状齿牙，玉
璇玑亦称玉牙璧，其几何形态的造型
极具动感，和谐而有韵律。

074 玉璇玑

直径 10.3~10.8 厘米　内径 6.3 厘米
厚 0.3~0.59 厘米

青绿玉质，温润细腻。体扁平，
局部绺裂处受沁有深褐色和灰白
色。孔壁打磨光滑规整，外缘有
三个形状相同、且均向同一方向
旋转的锯齿状齿牙，边缘呈刃状。

075 玉璇玑

外径 11.1 厘米　内径 6.65~7 厘米
厚 0.68 厘米

青白玉质，温润细腻。体扁平，
局部绺裂处受沁有深褐色和灰白
色。孔壁打磨圆滑，外缘有三个
形状相同、且均向同一方向旋转
的锯齿状齿牙，有打磨痕迹。

076 玉璇玑

直径 12.3~12.7 厘米　内径 6.3 厘米　厚 0.5 厘米
青黄玉质，体扁平。局部受沁呈灰白色。孔壁
打磨平滑，外缘有三个形状相同、且均向同一
方向旋转的齿牙，边缘打磨成刃状。

077 玉璇玑

直径 13.6~13.79 厘米　内径 5.98~6.45 厘米
厚 0.55 厘米

青黄玉质，较为温润。体扁平，局部受
沁有灰褐色。孔壁打磨圆滑规整，外缘
有两个相同锯齿状凸起的雏形及钻孔定
位痕。

078 玉璇玑

直径 15.7~16 厘米　内径 7~7.19 厘米　厚 0.36 厘米
白玉质，玉质温润剔透，局部绺裂处受沁呈褐色。
体扁平，玉璇玑中央有圆孔，孔壁打磨圆滑，形似
变形的环。外缘有三个形状相同、且均向同一方向
旋转的锯齿状齿牙。

079 玉璇玑与铜环组合器

直径 8.7~12.9 厘米　内径 6.8 厘米　厚 0.42~0.55 厘米
铜环 直径 10.5~10.8 厘米　内径 6.6~6.7 厘米　厚 0.1~0.2 厘米
青白玉质，温润剔透。体扁平，局部受沁呈褐色和灰白色。
孔壁打磨圆滑，外缘有三个形状相同、且均向同一方向旋
转的齿牙，齿牙处有砣治痕迹，有人工切割痕迹，器表遗
留有铜锈痕迹。这组璇玑与带齿铜环同出，铜环表面附着
有纺织物痕迹，玉璇玑与铜齿环的配套组合也是目前仅见，
对进一步研究玉璇玑的使用提供了新的思路。

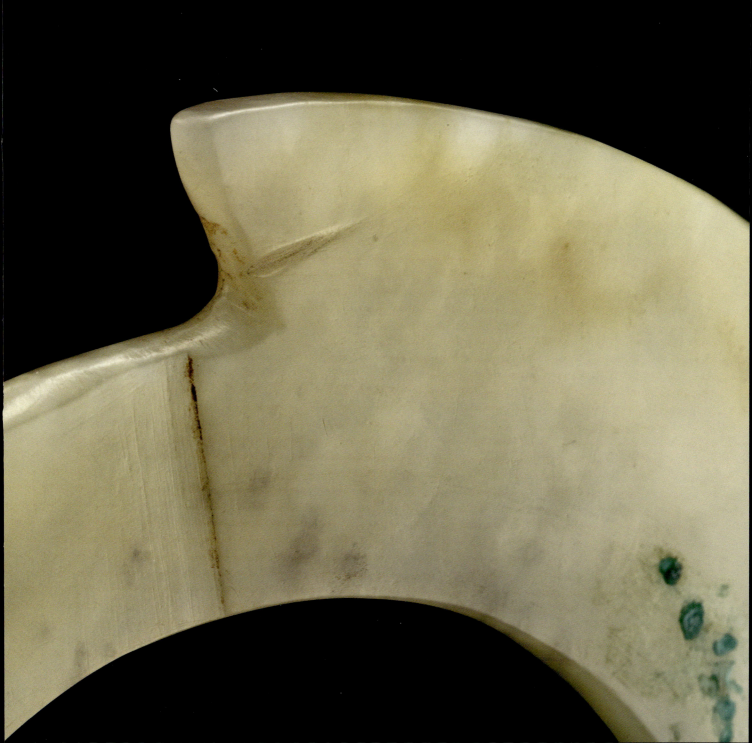

080 玉璇玑

直径 13.3~13.5 厘米　内径 6.4~6.45 厘米
厚 0.58~0.78 厘米

青黄玉质，温润细腻。体扁平，局部绺
裂处受沁呈深褐色和灰白色。孔壁打磨
圆滑，外缘有三个形状相同、且均向同
一方向旋转的齿牙。整体造形厚重大方。

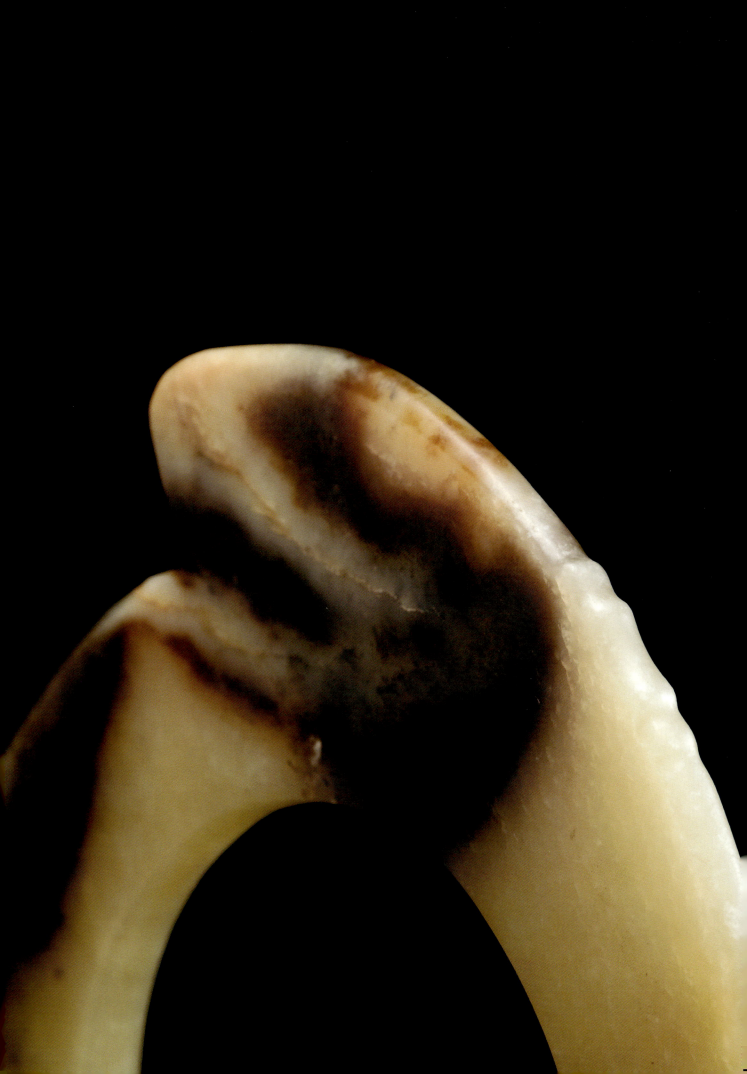

081 玉璇玑

直径 11.1~11.6 厘米　内径 6.4~6.6 厘米
厚 0.3~0.6 厘米

青黄玉质，温润剔透，玉质精良。体扁平，局部受沁呈褐色和灰白色。外缘有三个形状相等的豁口以代表齿牙，体现出同时期璇玑的又一种风格，内外壁打磨平整光滑。

082 玉璇玑

直径 11~11.2 厘米　内径 6.4 厘米　厚 0.4 厘米

青黄玉质，玉质精良，温润细腻。体扁平，孔壁打磨光滑。外缘雕琢有三组相同冠状扉牙，形似鸟类头部，玉质精纯，抛光极佳。

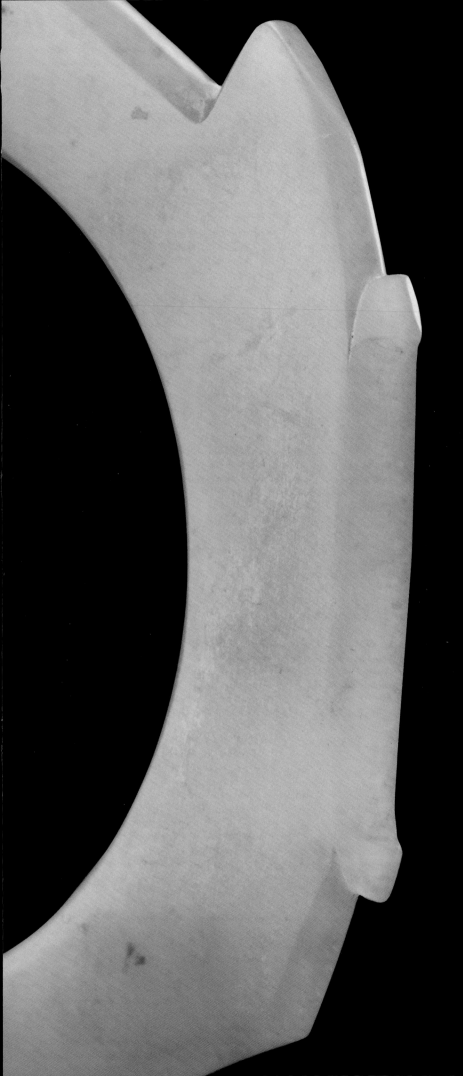

083 玉璇玑

直径 12.4~12.47 厘米　内径 7.35~7.45 厘米
厚 0.49 厘米

青黄玉质，温润细腻。体扁平，局部受
沁呈褐色和灰白色。孔壁打磨圆滑，外
缘有三组形状相同锯齿状扉棱。造型别
致新颖，是石峁玉璇玑的又一品种。

084 玉璇玑

直径 8.2~11.2 厘米　内径 6 厘米
厚 0.5 厘米

青白玉质，温润细腻。体扁平，局部受沁呈
灰白色和褐色。孔壁打磨光滑，外缘有三个
形状相同、且均向同一方向旋转的齿牙，齿
牙之间在齿牙有三组形状相同的扉棱。

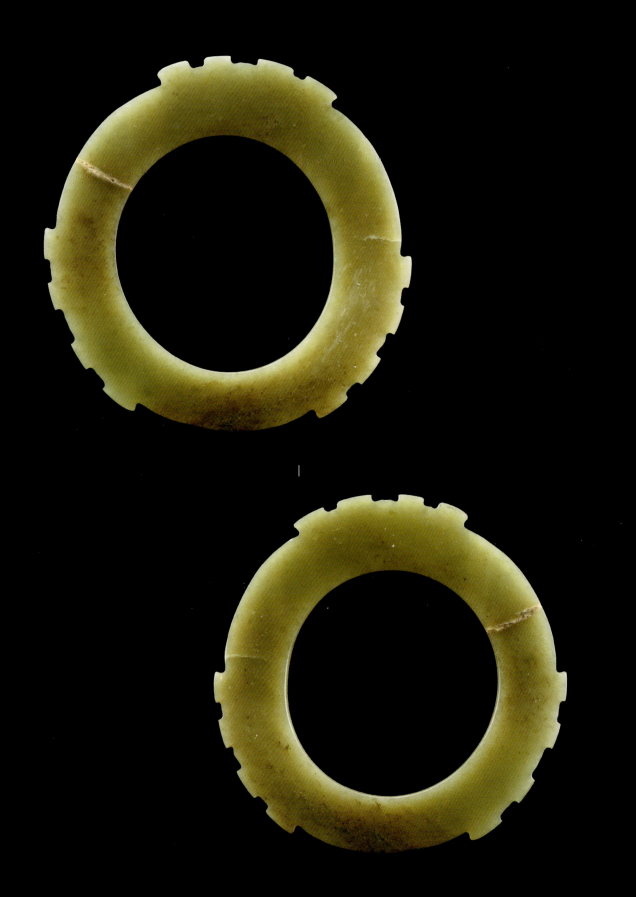

085 玉璇玑

直径 10.02~10.2 厘米　内径 6.25~6.4 厘米　厚 0.25~0.45 厘米

青黄玉质，温润剔透。体扁平，局部绺裂处受沁呈褐色。
孔壁打磨圆滑，外缘有三组形状相同的锯齿状扉棱。

086 玉璇玑

直径 16~16.2 厘米　内径 9.98~10.8 厘米　厚 0.6 厘米
青白玉质，温润细腻。体扁平，局部绺裂处受沁
呈褐色。孔壁打磨呈刃状，外缘有三组形状相同
的扉棱。

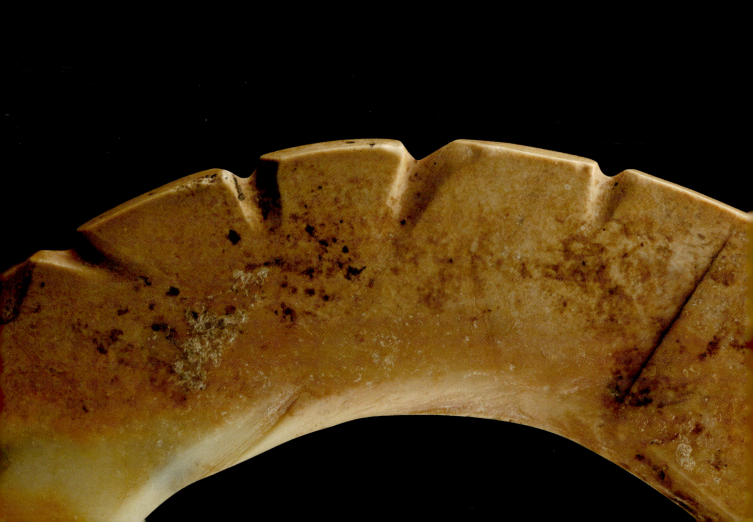

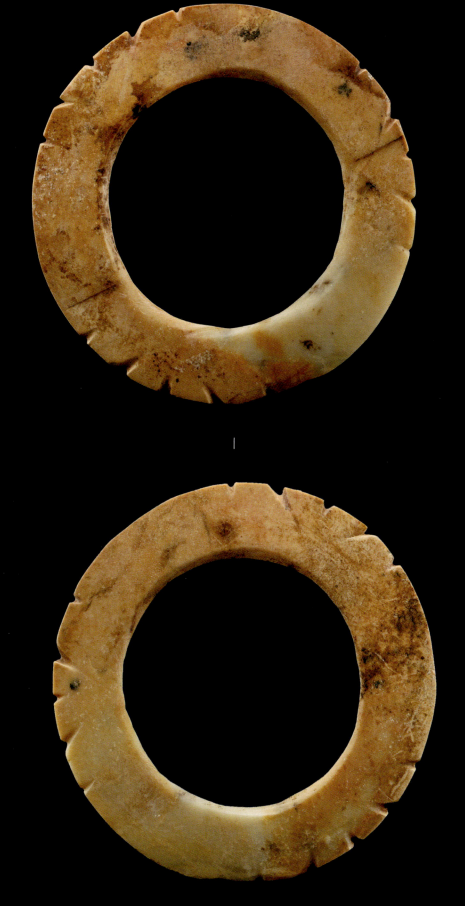

087 玉璇玑

直径 11.5~12.9 厘米　内径 7.2~7.5 厘米
厚 0.45~0.55 厘米

青黄玉质，温润剔透。有三个带扉棱玉璜组成，
玉璜两端各有孔穿系，外缘有三个形状相同、且
均向同一方向旋转的锯齿状凸起，在凸起之间雕
出三组相同的扉棱。石峁玉器中玉璇玑所用玉料
较其他器形更佳，这件璇玑玉质温润精纯，工艺
极富特点，充分体现了石峁玉器的高超水平。

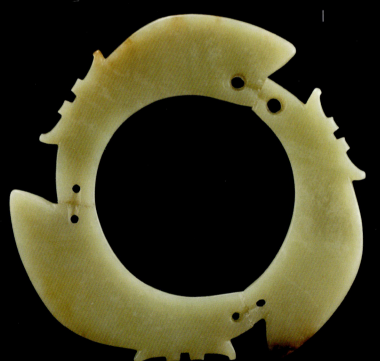

该璇玑形制十分特殊、为目前仅见。由三个相同
的带脊齿玉璜连缀组成，璜外缘对称的扉牙与石
峁遗址出土牙璋相似，各璜间以牙孔相连，分开
后又独立成三件玉璜，可谓匠心独运。玉质之佳
也是石峁玉器中十分罕见的，完全可媲美优质和
田籽玉。

088 玉璇玑

长 12.19~12.4 厘米　宽 10.15~10.65 厘米
内径 6.07~6.43 厘米　厚 0.1~0.55 厘米

青黄玉质，温润剔透。体扁平，呈长方形，局
部受沁呈褐色及灰白色，孔壁打磨圆滑。外缘
有三个形状相同、且均向同一方向旋转的齿牙，
在齿牙之间雕出三组不等的扉棱。

089 玉璇玑

长 11.7 厘米　宽 8.4~9.7 厘米

内径 6.07~6.43 厘米　厚 0.6 厘米

青白玉质,温润细腻。体扁平,呈长方形,局部受沁呈褐色和灰白色。
孔壁打磨圆滑,外缘有四个形状相同、且均向同一方向旋转的齿牙,
与山西清凉寺庙底沟二期遗址出土璇玑相似,边缘磨成刃状。

090 玉璇玑

直径 14.8 厘米　内径 6.6~6.92 厘米
厚 0.55~0.8 厘米

青玉质，温润剔透。体扁平，局部绺裂处受沁呈褐色和灰白色。孔壁打磨圆滑，外缘有三个形状相同、且均向同一方向旋转的齿牙，在齿牙之间雕出三组相同的扉棱。表面有人工切割痕迹。

091 玉璇玑

直径 13.4 厘米　内径 7.04 厘米　厚 0.5 厘米

青黄玉质，温润细腻。体扁平，局部受沁呈灰褐色和
灰白色点状。孔壁打磨圆滑，外缘有三个形状相同、
且均向同一方向旋转的齿牙，在齿牙之间雕出三组相
同的扉棱。表面有人工切割痕迹。

092 玉璇玑

直径 12.2　内径 5.7　厚 0.2~0.3 厘米

青白玉质，温润细腻。体扁平，局部受沁呈灰色和褐色。
孔壁打磨光滑，外缘有三个形状相同、且均向同一方向旋
转的齿牙，齿牙之间有三组形状相同的扉棱，抛光较好。

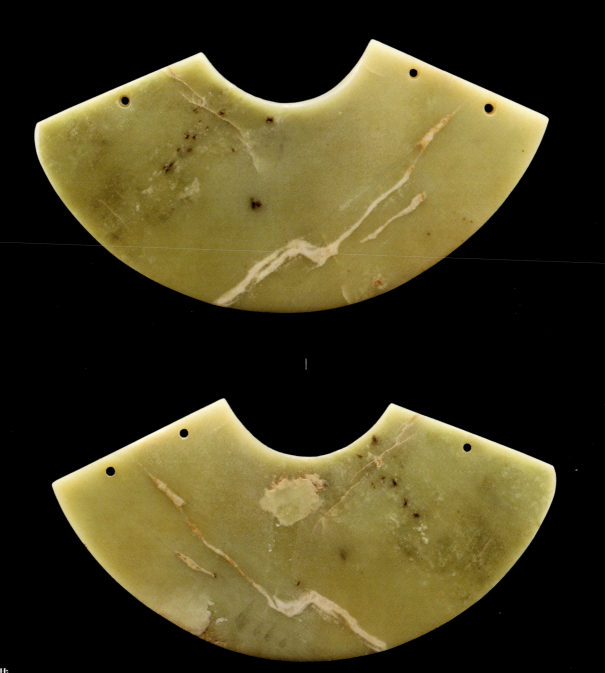

093 玉 璜

长 17.45 厘米　宽 6.62~6.92 厘米　厚 0.32~0.52 厘米

青黄玉质，细腻莹润。扁平弧形，呈扇面状，表面光素
无纹，局部绺裂处受沁呈褐色和灰白色。两端有单面钻孔，
其中一端为两孔，疑似联璜璧的一部分。

094 玉 璜

长 9.3 厘米　宽 2.6 厘米　厚 0.4 厘米

青玉质。扁平弧形，呈扇面状，表面光
素无纹，局部受沁呈鸡骨白色。两端有
单面钻孔，有人工切割痕迹。

095 玉 璜

长 4.6~8.9 厘米　宽 3.39~3.5 厘米　厚 0.31~0.57 厘米
青黄玉质，较为温润。扁平弧形，呈扇面状，表面
光素无纹，局部受沁呈灰白色。两端有孔，其中一
端有破损。

096 玉 璜

长 10.45 厘米　宽 2.2~2.85 厘米　厚 0.45 厘米
黄绿玉质，温润细腻。扁平弧形，呈不规则扇
面状，表面光素无纹，局部受沁呈灰白色。两
端为单面钻孔，有人工切割和打磨痕迹。

097 玉璜

长 10.28 厘米　宽 2.05~2.6 厘米　厚 0.32~0.5 厘米

黄绿玉质，温润细腻。扁平弧形，呈不规则扇面状，表面光
素无纹，局部受沁呈褐色和灰白色。一端有两个单面钻孔痕，
有人工十字形切割和打磨痕迹。整体形似鸟首。

098 玉 璜

长 11.5 厘米　宽 3.5 厘米　厚 0.4 厘米
青黄玉质，较为温润。扁平弧形，呈
扇面状，表面光素无纹，局部受沁呈
褐色和灰白色。两端单面钻孔，其中
一角有残缺。

099 玉　璜

长 11.89 厘米　宽 2.92 厘米　厚 0.25~0.43 厘米

青白玉质，黑色条纹，细腻莹润。扁平弧形，呈扇面状，
表面光素无纹，表面受沁呈褐色和灰白色。两端有
单面钻孔，外缘处有一稍大单面钻孔痕。

100 玉 璜

长 8.09 厘米　宽 1.3~1.69 厘米　厚 0.62 厘米

白玉质，细腻莹润，透亮有光泽。扁平弧形，呈扇面状，表
面光素无纹，局部受沁呈褐色。一端有孔，一端呈断裂状，
边缘较薄。

101 玉 璜

长 7.3 厘米　宽 2 厘米　厚 0.3 厘米

青白玉质，细腻莹润，透亮有光泽。扁平弧形，呈扇
面状，表面光素无纹，局部受沁呈褐色。两端有单面
钻孔。

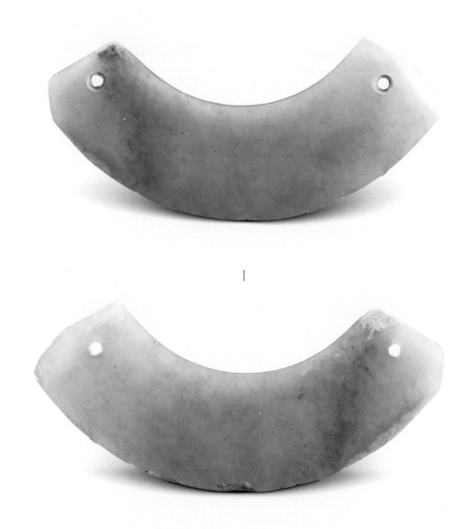

102 璜形器

长 13.65 厘米　宽 3.8~5.1 厘米　厚 0.45~0.58 厘米

青白玉质，莹润细腻。呈典型的不规则扇面状，表面光素无纹，局部受沁呈褐色和灰白色。两端有四个单面钻孔。

六 玉 斧

103 玉 斧

长 20.3 厘米　宽 5.7~7.4 厘米　厚 1.5 厘米

青黑玉质，杂质较多，石性较重。弧刃，双面磨刃，表面受沁呈灰白色和褐色。近首部有一单面钻孔，首部未加工。

104 玉 斧

长 25 厘米 宽 4.4~5.4 厘米 厚 1.2 厘米
青绿玉质，温润细腻。近似于椭圆形，
弧刃，双面磨刃，表面受沁呈灰白色
和褐色。首部呈弧形，近首部有两个
单面钻孔，其中一孔未钻透。

105 玉 斧

长 16.5 厘米　宽 5.2 厘米　厚 0.6 厘米

青黄玉质，温润细腻。通体平直，双面磨刃，
表面受沁呈灰白色和褐色。首部粗糙未加工，
近首部有一单面钻孔。

106 玉 斧

长 15.5 厘米　宽 3.8~4.81 厘米
厚 0.6 厘米

黄玉质，黑色斑点状沁色。通体扁平近
似于长方形，直刃，双面磨刃，近首部
有一喇叭状钻孔，首部残缺，未做加工。

107 玉 斧

长 14.7 厘米　宽 3.7~4.4 厘米　厚 0.6 厘米

青黄玉质,细腻温润。通体扁平近似于长方形,弧刃,双面磨刃,
表面受沁呈灰白色和墨绿色。首部平直,近首部有一单面钻孔。

108 玉　斧

长 16.7 厘米　宽 4.2~4.8 厘米　厚 0.9 厘米

青白玉质，黑色条纹状纹理，温润细腻。通体扁平近似于
长方形，直刃，单面磨刃，表面受沁呈褐色。首部平直，
未打孔，侧面有人工切割痕迹。

109 玉 斧

长 18.7 厘米　宽 4.5~5.2 厘米　厚 0.9 厘米

青绿玉质，温润透亮。双面磨弧刃，表面受沁呈灰白
色。首部稍作磨平，近首部有一单面钻孔，孔上方有
一未钻通柽钻孔，表面有人工切割痕迹。

110 玉　斧

长 24.5 厘米　宽 4.4~5 厘米　厚 0.6 厘米
青灰玉质，较为温润。通体扁平近似
于长方形，直刃，双面磨刃，表面受
沁呈灰白色和褐色。整体平直，近首
部有一单面钻孔。

111 玉 斧

长 13.1 厘米　宽 4.5~5 厘米　厚 1 厘米

青玉质。通体扁平近似于长方形，弧刃，双面磨刃，表面受沁呈灰白色和褐色。首部平直，近首部有一喇叭状钻孔。

112 玉 斧

长15.3厘米 宽3.7~5厘米 厚2.3厘米
青黑玉质,温润细腻。通体扁平近似于
长方形,弧刃,双面磨刃。首部粗糙未
加工,侧面有人工切割痕迹。

113 玉 斧

长 12.2 厘米　宽 3.65~5.22 厘米
厚 0.98 厘米
青玉质，玉质石性较重。通体扁平近似于长方形，弧刃，
双面磨刃，表面受沁呈灰白色。近首部有一喇叭状钻孔。

斧

米　宽 3.2~4.1 厘米　厚 1.2 厘米

。通体扁平近似于长方形，弧刃，双面磨刃，表面

白色和红褐色。首部平直，近首部有一单面钻孔。

115 玉 斧

长 22.3 厘米 宽 5.75~6.83 厘米 厚 0.9 厘米

黄玉质，杂质较多，通体扁平近似于长方形，平刃，
单面磨刃，表面受沁呈灰白色和褐色。首部平直，近
首部有一单面钻孔。

116 玉 斧

长 14 厘米 宽 4.7~7.8 厘米 厚 1.4 厘米

青黄玉质。通体扁平。双面磨弧刃，表面受沁呈灰白色和
黑褐色。首部呈弧形，近首部有两个单面钻孔。

117 玉 斧

长 12.4 厘米　宽 3.9~5.7 厘米　厚 1.1 厘米

黄绿玉质，温润细腻。双面磨刃，表面受沁呈
灰白色。首部弧形，近首部有一单面钻孔。

119 玉 斧

长 17 厘米　宽 9.6~10.4 厘米　厚 0.8 厘米
玉质已通体受沁呈鸡骨白色。通体扁平近似于长
方形，弧刃，双面磨刃，首部粗糙，未加工。近
首部有一单面钻孔。

121 玉 斧

长 12.6 厘米　宽 4.3~5.2 厘米　厚 1.4 厘米
受沁成鸡骨白色。通体扁平近似于长方形，
弧刃，双面磨刃，近首部有两个对钻孔。

七 玉 钺

122 玉 钺

长 15.4 厘米　宽 7.5~8.1 厘米　厚 0.32 厘米

上孔 1.15~1.35 厘米　下孔 1.5~1.6 厘米

青黄玉质，温润透亮。双面磨弧刃，表面受沁呈黑色和深褐色。近首处
有两个单面钻孔。

123 玉 钺

长 12 厘米　宽 8.22~8.32 厘米
厚 0.19~0.42 厘米

青玉质，温润细腻。通体扁平近似于长方形，首
部平直，弧刃，双面磨刃，表面受沁呈灰白色和
墨色。近首处有单面钻孔，刃部有单面钻孔痕迹。

124 玉 钺

长 11.4 厘米　宽 7.04~8 厘米　厚 0.5 厘米
孔径 1.65~2.0 厘米

青黄玉质，温润细腻。通体扁平近似于
长方形，首部平直，弧刃，双面磨刃，
表面受沁有褐色和灰白色，近首处有单
面钻孔，首部有残留有一大单面钻孔。

125 玉 钺

长 14.3 厘米　宽 8.0 厘米　厚 1.0 厘米

青绿玉质，温润细腻。通体扁平近似于长方形，直刃，双面磨刃，表面受沁呈灰白色和黑色。首部平直，近首部有一单面钻孔。

126 玉 钺

长 8.95 厘米　宽 6.82~7.02 厘米　厚 0.3 厘米
黄绿玉质，玉质较差。通体扁平近似于长方形，
首部稍有弧形，直刃，单面磨刃，表面受沁呈墨
色和灰白色。近首处有单面钻孔。

127 玉 钺

长 23 厘米 宽 9.32~13.71 厘米

厚 0.56 厘米

青玉质，受沁较重。通体扁平近似于长方形，首部平直，直刃，

128 玉 钺

长 12.7 厘米　宽 6.88~8.12 厘米　厚 0.2 厘米

青白玉质，玉质较疏松。通体扁平近似于长方形，
首部弧形，弧刃，单面磨刃，表面受沁呈深褐色。
近首处有单面钻孔，有破损。

129 玉 钺

长 11.8 厘米　宽 4.23~6.75 厘米　厚 0.52 厘米

玉质通体受沁呈鸡骨白化。通体扁平近似于长方形，首部弧形，

直刃，双面磨刃，近首处钻孔为对钻，刃部有破损。

130 玉 钺

长 13.2 厘米　宽 7.8~8.9 厘米　厚 0.3 厘米

黄绿玉质，温润细腻。双面磨直刃，通体较薄，表面受沁
呈灰褐色和土黄色。近背部有一喇叭状单面钻孔。

131 玉 钺

长 12.2 厘米 宽 8.1 厘米 厚 0.5 厘米

青绿玉质，杂质较多。双面磨直刃，表面受沁呈
褐色和灰白色。近首部有一个单面钻孔，表面有
人工切割痕迹，刃部有残缺。

132 玉 钺

长 12 厘米　宽 6.2~7.3 厘米　厚 0.6 厘米

青黄玉质。通体扁平近似于长方形，弧刃，双面
磨刃，表面受沁呈黄褐色和灰白色。首部平直，
近首部有一喇叭状钻孔。

133 玉 钺

长 12.79 厘米　宽 5.55~7.15 厘米

厚 0.07~0.17 厘米

黄绿玉质，温润细腻。通体打磨平整，双面磨直刃，通
体较薄，由牙璋改制而成，表面受沁呈黑色。近首部有
一喇叭状钻孔。此钺是石峁玉钺中最薄的一件，充分体
现了石峁玉器高超的打磨切割技术。

134 玉　钺

长 12.8 厘米　宽 6.3~6.8 厘米　厚 0.2 厘米

青黄玉质，温润细腻。双面磨弧刃，通体较薄，表面
受沁呈深褐色和灰白色。近首部有一喇叭状钻孔，刃
部有残缺。

135 玉 钺

长 10.5 厘米　宽 5.8~6.5 厘米　厚 0.3 厘米

青绿玉质，温润细腻。通体扁平近似于长方形，弧刃，
双面磨刃，表面受沁呈灰白色。背部平直，近背部有
一单面钻孔，有人工切割痕，为改制器。

136 玉　钺

137 玉 钺

长 8.3 厘米　宽 5.6 厘米　厚 0.5 厘米

青玉质。通体扁平近似于长方形，弧刃，单面磨刃，
表面受沁呈灰白色。首部平直，表面有三道凹槽，另
一面有一道凹槽。近首部有一单面钻孔。

138 玉 钺

长 8.55 厘米　宽 3.56~4.71 厘米
厚 0.4 厘米
青白玉质，温润细腻。通体扁平近似于长方
形，平刃，双面磨刃，通体较薄，表面受沁
呈黄褐色和灰黑色。近首部有一喇叭状钻孔。

140 玉 钺

长 10.68 厘米　宽 4.25~4.8 厘米　厚 0.5 厘米

青黄玉质，温润细腻。通体扁平近似于长方形，双面磨刃，表面受沁呈灰白色和褐色，首部平直，近首部有一单面钻孔。

141 玉 钺

长 18.9 厘米　宽 7.98~9.65 厘米
厚 0.63 厘米

青黄玉质，纵向条带状纹理。通体扁平近似于长
方形，直刃，双面磨刃，表面受沁呈灰褐色。近
首部有一喇叭状钻孔。

142 玉 钺

长 15.2 厘米　宽 7.9~8.9 厘米　厚 0.65 厘米

青白玉质。通体扁平近似于长方形，直刃，双面磨刃，表面受沁呈土黄色和灰白色。首部平直，近首部有一喇叭状钻孔。

143 玉 钺

长 14.8 厘米　宽 7~7.8 厘米　厚 0.5 厘米

青绿玉质，玉质较差。通体扁平近似于长方形，直刃，双面磨
刃，表面受沁呈黑褐色和灰白色。首部呈弧形，近首部有双面
对钻孔，表面有残断。

144 玉 钺

长 19 厘米　宽 9.5~10.7 厘米　厚 0.4 厘米

青玉质,较为温润。双面磨直刃,表面受沁呈灰白色。
近首部有一喇叭状钻孔,有人工切割痕,为明显的
改制器。

145 玉 钺

长 10.2 厘米　宽 7.5~8.4 厘米　厚 0.3 厘米

青白玉质。通体扁平近似于长方形，弧刃，双面磨刃，表
面受沁呈灰白色和墨绿色。首部平直，近首部有一喇叭状
钻孔，首部有残缺。

146 玉 钺

长 14.4 厘米　宽 6.5~7.4 厘米　厚 0.5 厘米

青绿玉质。通体扁平近似于长方形，弧刃，双面磨刃，
表面受沁呈灰白色和褐色。首部呈三角形，近首部有
一喇叭状钻孔。

一

147 玉 钺

长 10.96 厘米　宽 3.75~4.49 厘米　厚 0.25 厘米

青绿玉质，温润透亮，透明度极高。通体扁平近似于
长方形，直刃，双面磨刃，通体较薄，表面受沁呈黑
色雪花状。近首部有一单面钻孔，首部有一缺口。

148 玉 钺

长 9.75 厘米　宽 3.9~5 厘米　厚 0.3 厘米

青黄玉质，较为温润。通体扁平近似于长方形、直刃、双面磨刃，表面受沁呈褐色和灰白色。近首部有一单面钻孔。

149 玉 钺

长 10.15 厘米　宽 5.21~6.1 厘米

厚 0.47 厘米

青绿玉质，杂质较多。通体扁平，近似于
长方形，弧刃，单面磨刃，表面受沁呈黑
色和灰白色。近首部有一单面钻孔。

150 玉 钺

长 10.6 厘米　宽 5.4~5.7 厘米　厚 0.45 厘米

青白玉质，温润细腻。通体扁平近似于长方形，弧刃，
单面磨刃，表面受沁呈褐色和灰白色。首部平直，近
首部有一双面对钻孔。

151 玉 钺

长 13 厘米　宽 4.7~5.2 厘米　厚 0.45 厘米

青白玉质，褐色条纹状纹理。通体扁平近似于长方形，弧
刃、双面磨刃，表面受沁呈灰白色和红褐色。首部平直，
近首部有一喇叭状钻孔。

八 玉 璋

153 玉 璋

长 13.02 厘米　宽 5.5~5.95 厘米　厚 0.15~0.3 厘米

深绿色玉质，温润细腻，通体扁平较薄，局部受沁呈
灰白色。仅存一小部分璋体和柄部，阑部有扉牙痕迹
及平行阴刻线，被片切割一分为二，背面光素，柄部
有一喇叭状穿孔。

154 玉　璋

长 21.1 厘米　宽 9.7~10.5 厘米　厚 0.5 厘米

玉质已通体受沁，表面呈灰白及浅褐色，有钙化剥落。
双面磨直刃，柄部平直，两侧有扉棱，近柄部有一单
面钻孔。

九 玉锛、凿

一

155 玉 锛

长 7.9 厘米 宽 1.5 厘米 厚 1.5 厘米

青绿玉质，温润细腻。通体近似于长方柱状体，
弧刃，双面磨刃，表面受沁呈灰白色和褐色。首
部粗糙未加工。

156 玉 锛

长 9.9 厘米　宽 2 厘米　厚 0.8 厘米

青白玉质。通体扁平近似于长方形，弧刃，双面磨刃，表面受沁呈灰白色，首部平直。

157 玉 锛

长 12.2 厘米　宽 1~1.9 厘米　厚 0.9 厘米

青白玉质，温润细腻。通体扁平近似于长方形，
中间宽两端稍窄，直刃，双面磨刃，表面受沁
呈灰白色和褐色，首部稍倾斜。

158 玉 凿

长 21.7 厘米　宽 2.6~2.9 厘米　厚 1.2 厘米
青绿玉质，杂质较多。弧刃，双面磨刃，
表面受沁呈红褐色和灰白色。首部有一对
钻孔，中部残断。

159 玉 凿

长 19.2 厘米 宽 3.1~3.3 厘米 厚 0.5 厘米

青绿玉质，温润细腻。通体扁平近似于长方形，直刃，双面磨刃，表面受沁呈褐色。留有切割的痕迹，首部平直，近首部有一单面钻孔。

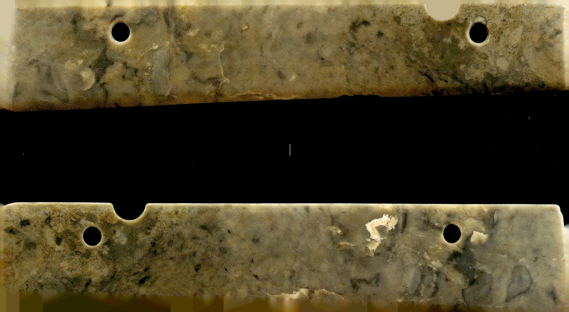

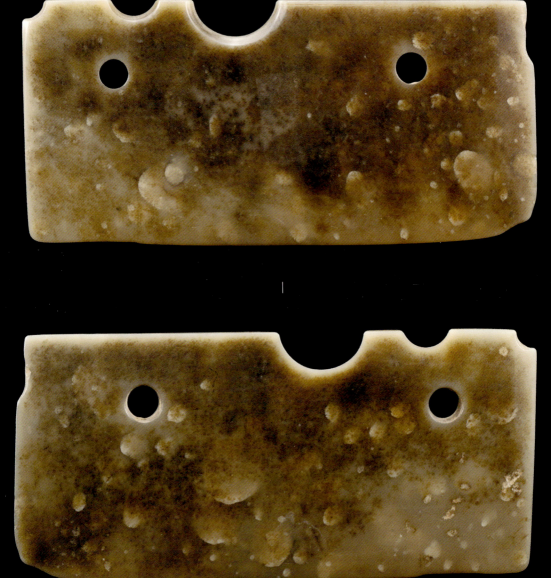

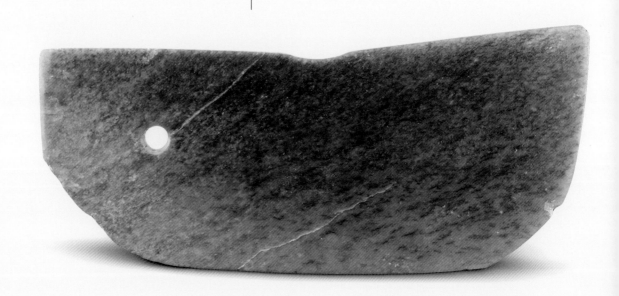

163 玉 刀

长 21.4 厘米　宽 8.1~8.9 厘米　厚 0.4 厘米

青绿玉质，杂质较多。略呈扇面状，表面受沁呈灰白色，刃口
双面斜磨成刃，背部平直。应为玉斧改制而成，背部有原器单
面钻孔痕迹，且有现器物的单面钻孔。

164 玉 刀

长 14.2 厘米　宽 5.7~6.7 厘米　厚 0.5 厘米
青白玉质，杂质较多。通体扁平近似于长方形，
弧刃，单面磨刃，表面受沁呈红褐色和灰白
色，背部平直。侧面有一原器单面钻孔痕迹。
表面有人工切割痕迹，背部有一单面钻孔。

青黄玉质，温润细腻。略呈长方形，表面受沁呈灰白色和红褐色，刃口双面斜磨成刃，背部平直。有人工切痕和单面钻孔痕，表面也留有人工切割痕迹，背部有一个单面钻孔。

166 玉　刀

长 14.1 厘米　宽 4~4.4 厘米　厚 0.4 厘米

青绿玉质，杂质较多。通体扁平近似于长方形，弧刃，双面磨刃，
表面受沁呈灰白色和褐色。应为原器 1/2 大，被纵向一分为二，
背部平直，近背部有一原斧单面钻孔。

167 玉　刀

长 18.2 厘米　宽 9.1 厘米　厚 0.4 厘米

青玉质，杂质较多，有浅灰色沁蚀痕迹。略呈长方形，
背部平直，三面磨刃，近背部居中有一圆形钻孔。

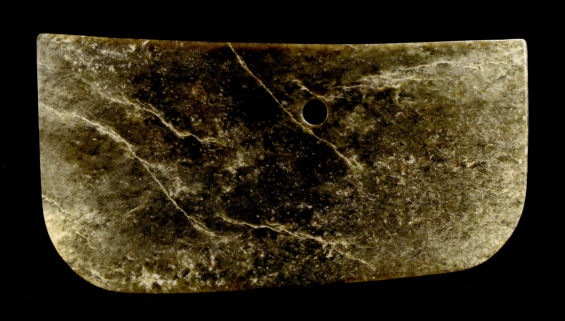

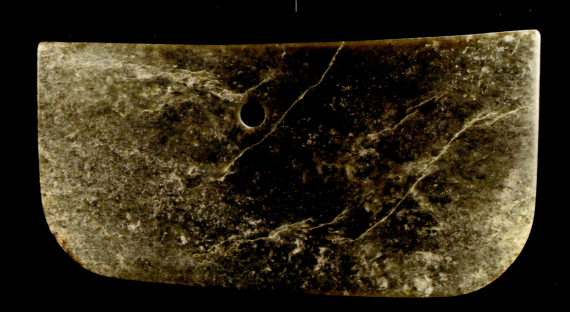

168 玉 刀

长 12.8 厘米　宽 2.4~2.9 厘米　厚 0.3 厘米

青黄玉质，杂质较多，受沁严重。通体扁平近似于长方形，弧刃，双面磨刃，表面受沁呈灰白色。应为原器 1/4 大，被横向、纵向一分为二，背部平直，近背部有一单面钻孔，有人工切割痕迹。

169 玉 刀

长 15.1 厘米　宽 2.6~2.9 厘米　厚 0.4 厘米

青黄玉质，较为温润。略呈长方形，表面受沁呈灰白色和深褐色，应为其他器物改制而成。未磨刃，侧面有原器单面钻孔痕迹，背部平直，有一个单面钻孔。

170 玉　刀

长 13 厘米　宽 3~3.9 厘米　厚 0.6 厘米

青黄玉质，温润细腻。通体扁平近似于长方形，弧刃，单面磨刃，表面受
沁呈灰白色和褐色，背部平直。应为原器 1/2 大，被纵向一分为二，侧面
有原器单面钻孔痕迹，有人工切割痕迹，背部有一单面钻孔。

171 双孔玉刀

长 15.6 厘米　宽 4.3~5 厘米　厚 0.7 厘米

青绿玉质，较为温润。三面磨刃，表面受沁呈灰白色。

中间单面钻孔为原玉刀孔，首部有一单面钻孔。

173 玉 刀

长 10.3 厘米　宽 2.3~2.9 厘米　厚 0.6 厘米

青黄玉质，玉质较差。通体扁平近似于长方形，
弧刃，双面磨刃，表面受沁呈灰白色。应为原器
1/2 大，被纵向一分为二，首部呈弧形，近首部
有一单面钻孔，有人工切割痕迹。

174 玉　刀

长 14.3 厘米　宽 4.6~5.2 厘米　厚 0.4 厘米

墨玉质，打磨光亮。单面磨斜刃，表面受沁呈灰白色和黄褐色，首
部呈刃状，近首部有一对钻孔。由 1/4 斧剖制而成，侧面留有原孔
一半的单面钻孔，有人工切割痕迹，首部有一单面钻孔，应为改制器。

175 玉 刀

长 12 厘米　宽 4.9~5.7 厘米　厚 0.3 厘米

青白玉质，温润细腻。通体扁平近似于长方形，弧刃，单面
磨刃，表面受沁呈褐色和黑色。两器为一件，被纵向一分为
二，近首部有一单面钻孔，首部未做细加工。该玉刀为改制
器，根据形制推断为由一件玉钺一分为四而成。

176 玉 刀

长 12.3 厘米　宽 3.7~3.9 厘米　厚 0.5 厘米

青玉质，温润细腻。通体扁平近似于长方形，直刃，
双面磨刃，表面受沁呈灰白色和褐色。首部粗糙未加
工，近首部有一单面钻孔。

177 玉 刀

长 9.2 厘米 宽 3.7~4 厘米 厚 0.4 厘米

青玉质。通体扁平近似于长方形，弧刃，双面磨刃，表面受沁呈灰白色。背部打磨成刃状，近背部和刃部各有一喇叭状钻孔，残断。

十一 玉 圭

178 玉 圭

长 35.5 厘米　宽 6.89~10.2 厘米　厚 0.7 厘米

青黄玉质，杂质较多。器形扁厚，尖首长条状，素面无纹，
表面受沁呈黑褐色和灰白色，边缘磨成刃状。柄部有一对钻
孔，表面有人工切割痕迹。

179 石 圭

长 26.85 厘米　宽 6.88~7.09 厘米
厚 0.73 厘米

玉质通体受沁呈灰白色和黄褐
色。器形扁厚，呈尖首长条状，
素面无纹，圭身平直光滑。

一

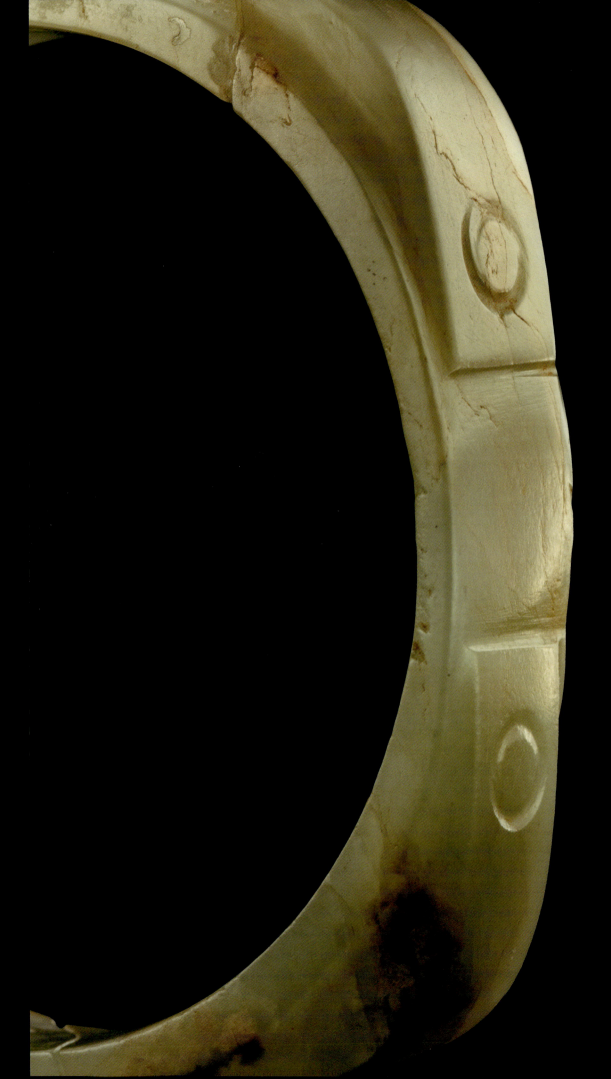

十二　玉　琮

180 玉　琮

长 7.1 厘米　宽 6.96 厘米　高 1.6~1.8 厘米
厚 0.25~1.03 厘米　孔径 6.3~6.7 厘米

青白玉质，温润细腻，色泽莹润。呈扁矮
方柱状，内圆外方，表面受沁呈褐色和灰
白色。四角各雕有一组人面纹，仅有一双
眼睛表示，原断为两截，两端有穿孔连缀，
有良渚玉器的特征。

181 玉 琮

长 5.3~5.6 厘米　宽 5.3~5.6 厘米　高 5.55 厘米　厚 0.2~1.69 厘米

上孔内径 4.9~5 厘米　上孔外径 5.4~5.6 厘米

下孔孔内径 4.85~4.95 厘米　下孔外径 5.6~5.7 厘米

青黄玉质，较为温润。呈扁矮方柱状，内圆外方，通体素面无纹，局部受沁呈黑褐色和灰白色。器型规整，厚薄均匀，边角端正，轮廓分明，具有齐家玉器风格特点。

182 玉 琮

长 7.97 厘米　宽 7.75 厘米　高 2.4 厘米
厚 0.15~1.55 厘米　孔径 6.22~7.3 厘米
青绿玉质，温润细腻。呈扁矮方柱状，内圆外方，通
体素面无纹，局部受沁呈黄褐色。器型规整，边角圆
滑，轮廓分明，有人工切割痕迹，有良渚玉器特点。

183 玉 琮

长 5.5 厘米　宽 5.3 厘米　高 3~3.12 厘米　厚 0.3~1.6 厘米
上孔内径 4.6~4.7 厘米　上孔外径 5.4~5.6 厘米
下孔内径 4.6 厘米　下孔外径 5.3~5.6 厘米
青黄玉质，较为温润。呈扁矮方柱状，内圆外方，通体
素面无纹，表面受沁严重呈深褐色和灰白色。器型规整，
边角端正。

184 玉 琮

长 4.98 厘米　宽 4.82 厘米　高 2.65~2.72 厘米
厚 0.2~1.2 厘米　孔径 4.2~5 厘米

青绿玉质，温润细腻。呈扁矮方柱状，内圆外方，通体
素面无纹，内圆外方，局部受沁呈深褐色和灰白色。器
形规整，边角打磨光滑。

185 玉　琮

长 4.98 厘米　宽 4.82 厘米　高 2.65~2.72 厘米

厚 0.2~1.2 厘米　孔径 4.2~5 厘米

青黄玉质，温润细腻。呈扁矮方柱状，通体素面无纹，
局部受沁呈深褐色和灰白色，有人工切割痕迹。

186 玉 琮

长 7.2 厘米　宽 7.04 厘米　高 9.6~9.8 厘米
厚 0.3~2.25 厘米　孔径 5.65~7 厘米

青黄玉质，较为温润。呈长方柱状，内圆外方，通体素面
无纹，局部绺裂处受沁呈黄褐色。器型规整，具有齐家文
化玉器风格。

187 玉 琮

长 7.97 厘米　宽 7.75 厘米　高 2.4 厘米

厚 0.15~1.55 厘米　孔径 6.22~7.3 厘米

青黄玉质，温润细腻。呈扁矮方柱状，内圆外方，通体素面
无纹，局部受沁呈黄褐色。器型规整，边角圆滑，轮廓分明，
有人工切割痕迹，有良渚文化玉器特征。

188 玉 琮

长 3.1 厘米　宽 3.2 厘米　高 5.2 厘米

厚 0.3~0.9 厘米　孔径 2.4~2.5 厘米

青黄玉质，温润细腻。呈长方柱状，通体素面无纹，局部
受沁呈深褐色和灰白色，有齐家文化玉器风格。

189 玉　琮

长 5.6 厘米　宽 4.7 厘米　高 2.94 厘米　孔径 4.9 厘米

青黄玉质，温润细腻。扁矮方柱状，内圆外方，通体
素面无纹，局部受沁呈黑褐色和灰白色。器型规整，
边角圆滑，有向内打洼呈束腰状处理，轮廓分明。

190 琮形器

长 8.1 厘米 宽 8.2 厘米 厚 0.4~0.7 厘米 高 1.9 厘米
孔径长 5.8~6.7 厘米 孔径宽 6.2~6.6 厘米
青绿彩石质，间以片状杂质。圆角方形，内外形状一致，
通体素面无纹，局部裂绺处受沁呈褐色和灰白色。

191 琮形器

长 7.2 厘米　宽 7.3 厘米　厚 0.5~1.9 厘米
孔径 5.8~6.1 厘米

青白玉质，温润细腻。外呈方形，内为圆孔，通体
素面无纹，局部绺裂处受沁呈褐色和灰白色。边角
打磨光滑。

192 琮形器

长 7.25 厘米　宽 7.18 厘米　厚 0.5~1.07 厘米

孔径 5.89~6.05 厘米　高 0.9~1.1 厘米

黄绿玉质，温润细腻。内圆外方，局部受沁呈褐色和
灰白色。外壁四角留有简化的兽面纹饰，为良渚文化
玉器的典型特征。

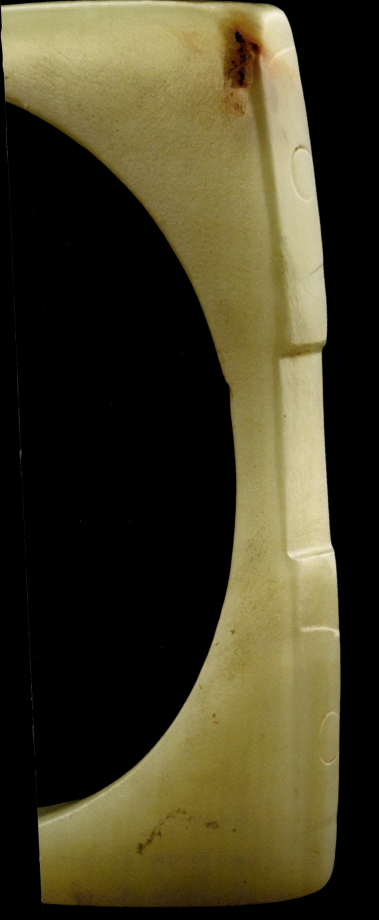

高 3.45 厘米　直径 2.5~3.1 厘米

青黄玉质，莹润细腻。呈圆台状，上宽下窄，局部受
沁呈褐色和灰白色。通身素面无纹，中部有对向旋切
留下的台痕，底部有一浅的钻痕。

194 束腰形器

直径 2.25~2.8 厘米　高 4.95 厘米　孔径 0.8 厘米（进深 0.15 厘米）

青黄玉质，莹润细腻，光泽甚佳。为亚腰状，两边粗大，中间束腰，
两端平整，素面无纹，局部受沁呈黄褐色，底部有一浅的钻痕。

195 玉 镯

直径 6.6~7.1 厘米　厚 0.3~0.45 厘米

高 1.2 厘米　内径 6.1~6.3 厘米

青黄玉质，温润细腻。椭圆筒形，局部受沁呈黄褐色和灰白色。
通体精磨抛光，边缘未进行磨圆处理，基本保持切割后形成的
棱角。外壁四角各留有一组半神人纹，帽子上有阴刻的细密纹
饰，鼻子为减地凸起，纹饰细如发丝，堪称微雕，具有典型的
良渚玉器特征。

196 玉 镯

高 1.5 厘米　外径 7.1 厘米　内径 6.4~6.6 厘米

青绿玉质，温润细腻。扁圆筒形，局部受沁呈灰白色。通体
精磨抛光，边缘未进行磨圆处理，外壁有八道竖向阴刻线。

197 玉 镯

高 1.9 厘米　外径 9.8 厘米　内径 8.3 厘米

青黄玉质，温润细腻。扁圆筒形，局部受沁呈深
褐色和灰白色。通体精磨抛光，边缘未进行磨圆
处理，基本保持切割后形成的棱角，外壁有四组
减地凸起，每个凸起有两组凹槽。

198 玉 镯

直径 8.6 厘米　内径 6.5 厘米　厚 0.85 厘米

青白玉质，温润细腻通透有光泽，犹如
凝脂。扁平圆环状，表面光素无纹。整
体圆整光洁，截面呈椭圆形，打磨精致，
有人工切割痕迹。

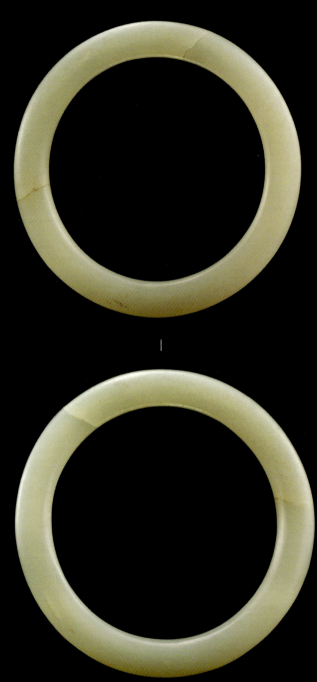

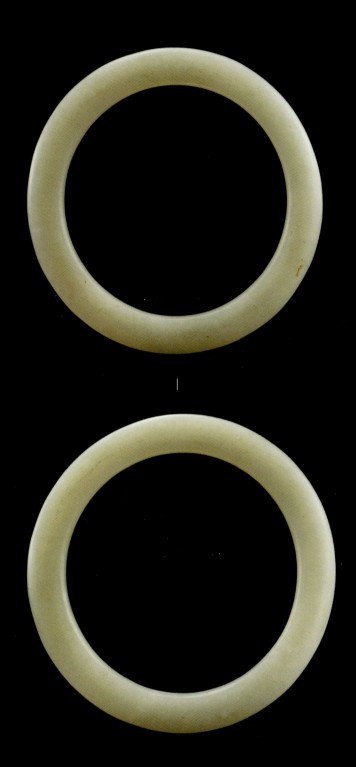

199 玉 镯

直径 9.45 厘米　内径 8.2~8.35 厘米　厚 0.7 厘米

青白玉质，温润细腻，玉质精纯。扁平圆环状，素面无纹，局部有灰白色沁。整体圆整光洁，内外壁平滑，通体磨光。

保持切割后形成的棱角，外壁有四组平行弦纹。

200 玉 镯

高 3.5 厘米　外径 8.3 厘米　内径 6.4 厘米

青绿玉质，温润细腻。圆筒形，局部受沁呈深褐色和
灰白色。通体精磨抛光，边缘未进行磨圆处理，基本
保持切割后形成的棱角，外壁有四组平行弦纹。

201 玉 镯

高 2.1~2.2 厘米　外径 7.7~8 厘米　内径 6.7~6.8 厘米

青白玉质，温润细腻。扁圆筒形，局部受沁呈褐色。通体
精磨抛光，边缘未进行磨圆处理，外壁有七道竖向阴刻线。

202 玉 镯

高 3.1 厘米　外径 8.2 厘米　内径 7.1 厘米

青绿玉质，温润细腻。圆筒形，局部受沁呈深褐色和灰白色。
通体精磨抛光，边缘未进行磨圆处理，基本保持切割后形成的
棱角，外壁有一圈平行的凹弦纹，底部有八道斜向的阴刻线。

203 玉 镯

高 4.3 厘米　外径 8.4~8.7 厘米　内径 7.1~7.3 厘米

青绿彩石质，有类似云母质斑，较细腻。圆筒形，通体素面
无纹，局部受沁呈深褐色和灰白色。通体精磨抛光，边缘未
进行磨圆处理，基本保持切割后形成的棱角。

204 玉 镯

高 3.1~3.3 厘米　外径 9.7 厘米　内径 8.2 厘米
青绿彩石质，有类似云母质斑，较细腻。圆
筒形，通体素面无纹，局部受沁呈深褐色和
灰白色。通体精磨抛光，边缘未进行磨圆处理，
基本保持切割后形成的棱角。

205 玉　镯

直径 8 厘米　高 2.1 厘米　厚 0.55~1.19 厘米

上口外径 7.69 厘米　下口外径 7.75 厘米

上口内径 5.51~6.07 厘米　下口内径 6.22~6.38 厘米

青黄玉质。扁圆筒状，局部受沁呈黄褐色。通身素面无纹，精
磨抛光，边缘未进行磨圆处理，基本保持切割后形成的棱角。

206 玉 镯

高 1.8~2.1 厘米　外径 7.9 厘米　厚 0.7~0.9 厘米　内径 6.2 厘米

青绿玉质，温润细腻。扁圆筒形，局部受沁呈黄褐色和灰白色。

通身素面无纹，此器为通体精磨抛光，边缘未进行磨圆处理，基

本保持切割后形成的棱角。

207 玉 镯

高 2.5 厘米　外径 5.9 厘米　内径 4.7 厘米
青黄玉质，温润细腻。扁圆筒形，局部受沁
呈黄褐色和灰白色，通体素面无纹。精磨抛光，
边缘未进行磨圆处理，基本保持切割后形成
的棱角。

208 束腰形玉镯

高 2.8 厘米　外径 5.8 厘米　内径 4.9 厘米

青玉质，温润细腻。呈束腰状，表面受沁呈土黄褐色，素面无纹。

通体精磨抛光，边缘未进行磨圆处理，基本保持切割后形成的棱角。

209 束腰形玉镯

高2.3厘米　外径5.4厘米　内径4.8厘米

红褐色玉质，温润细腻。呈束腰状，表面受沁呈土黄褐色，素面无纹。通体精磨抛光，边缘未进行磨圆处理，基本保持切割后形成的棱角。

210 玉 镯

高 2.3 厘米　外径 7.8 厘米　内径 7.2 厘米

青玉质，温润细腻。扁圆筒形，局部受沁呈黄褐色和灰白色，
通体精磨抛光。边缘未进行磨圆处理，基本保持切割后形成的
棱角。八道竖向阴刻线分成四组，每组中间有一镂空十字。

211 束腰形玉镯

高 4.1 厘米　外径 7.3 厘米　内径 6.6 厘米

青玉质，玉质较为温润。呈束腰状，表面受沁呈褐色
和灰白色，素面无纹。通体磨制光滑，边缘未进行磨
圆处理，基本保持切割后形成的棱角。

212 玉 镯

高 3.3 厘米　外径 8.3 厘米　内径 6.7 厘米

青白玉质，温润细腻。圆筒形，局部受沁呈灰白色和
褐色，通体精磨抛光，边缘未进行磨圆处理，基本保
持切割后形成的棱角，外壁有三圈平行的凹弦纹。

213 玉柄形器

长 18.4 厘米　宽 0.75~1.3 厘米　厚 0.6~0.88 厘米

黄玉质，温润透亮。扁平长方体，通身素面无纹，局部受沁呈褐色和灰白色。由柄首、柄身构成，柄首呈束腰状，柄身

214 玉柄形器

长 16.3 厘米　宽 0.97~2.23 厘米　厚 0.17~0.55 厘米

青白玉质，细腻温润。扁平长方体片状，通身素面无纹，局部受沁呈黄色和灰白色。由柄首、柄身构成，柄首呈束腰形，末端为不规则状。

215 玉柄形器

长 11.2 厘米　宽 2.3~3 厘米　厚 0.1~0.2 厘米

青玉质，温润细腻。扁平长方体片状，通身素面无纹，
局部受沁呈深褐色和灰白色。由柄首、柄身构成，
柄首呈束腰形，末端为不规则状，有人工切割痕迹。

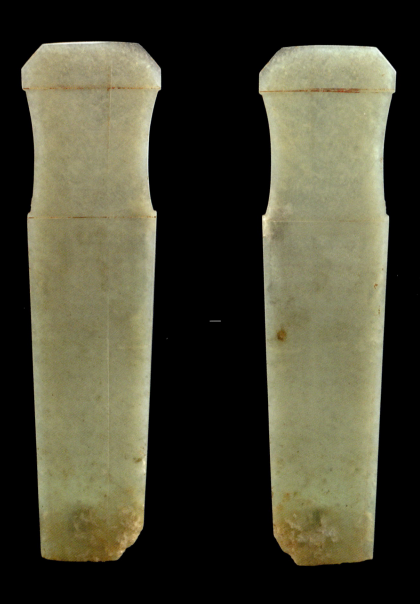

216 玉柄形器

长 9.31 厘米　宽 2.9~3.25 厘米　厚 0.29 厘米

青玉质，温细腻润。扁平长方体片状，通身素面无纹，
局部受沁呈灰白色。由柄首、柄身构成，柄首呈束腰形，
柄首较长，柄身下半部被裁截，仅留上半段柄身。

217 玉柄形器

长 6.8 厘米　宽 3.25~3.49 厘米　厚 0.23~0.4 厘米

青白玉质，温润细腻。扁平长方体片状，通身素面无纹，
局部受沁呈黑色点状。由柄首、柄身构成，柄首呈束腰形，
柄首较长，柄身下半部被裁截，仅留上半段柄身。

218 玉柄形器

长 10 厘米　宽 2.3~2.6 厘米　厚 0.35 厘米

青白玉质，细腻温润。扁平长方体片状，通身素面无纹，局部受沁呈褐色。仅留柄身，末端留有不规则状残留，表面有人工切割痕迹，柄身有一孔，镶嵌有绿松石圆片。

219 玉柄形器

长 8.2 厘米　宽 0.55~1.62 厘米　厚 0.65 厘米

黄玉质，温润细腻。扁平长方体片状，通身素面无纹，局部受沁呈灰白色。由柄首、柄身构成，末端为凸榫状，有一喇叭形穿孔，柄首隐约可见束腰形，两面和柄首被打磨光滑似弧形。

220 玉人面像

高 3.85 厘米 宽 3.8 厘米 厚 0.6 厘米

青白玉质，温润细腻，侧面人像，鹰钩鼻、大眼，面部有一
单面穿孔，月牙形耳，头部有一小单面钻孔。该人面像是
石峁文化的代表图案，常见于石雕、陶器等器物上。玉制人
面像目前仅发现二件，另一件现藏于陕西省历史博物馆。

221 鱼形玉佩

长 6 厘米　宽 3.05 厘米　厚 0.1~0.9 厘米

白玉质，莹润细腻，透亮纯净。眼睛为一单面钻孔，尾为弧形，原始的线切割雕琢成蝌蚪纹，活灵活现，雕琢细致。

222 透雕形玉簪首

长 6.45 厘米　宽 6.7 厘米　厚 0.3 厘米

青黄玉质，温润柔和，透亮纯净。沁色过度自然，用原始的线切割镂空雕琢出冠状纹饰，具有山东龙山文化玉器和石家河文化玉器风格。

223 高冠侧身玉人像

长 6.8 厘米　宽 2.05~2.1 厘米　厚 3.5~7.5 厘米
青白玉质，莹润细腻，透亮纯净。用简化的侧身做成
人蹲踞状，头戴高冠，透雕部分以原始的线切割制成，
前肢下垂。

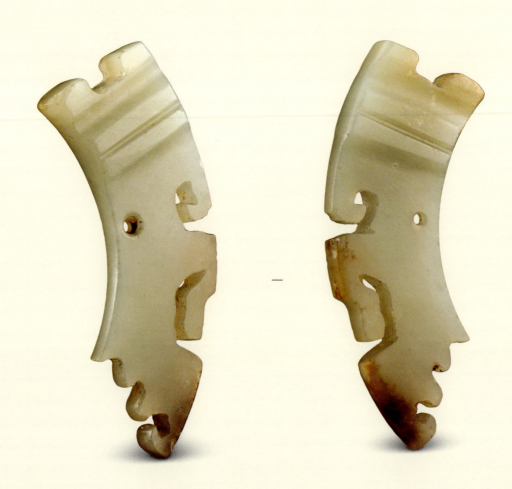

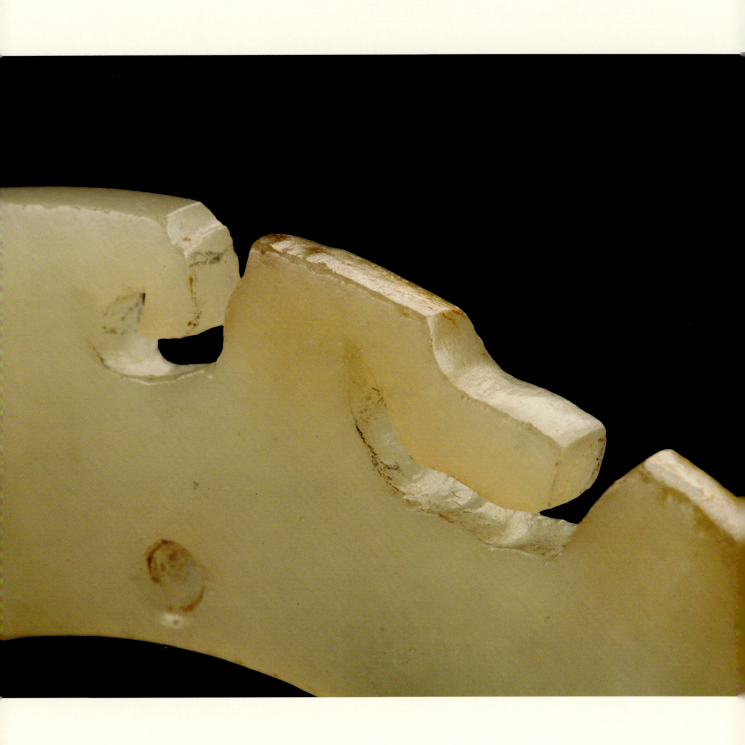

224 对鸟形玉佩

长 7.5 厘米　宽 5.9 厘米　厚 0.21 厘米

青玉质，温润柔和。用钻孔和砣具镂空透雕出相背而立的两只鸟，鸟作回首展翅状，局部受沁呈褐色和灰白色，沁色过度自然，上部有一钻孔，作为穿系佩戴用。

225 对兽形玉佩

长 7.5 厘米　宽 3.9 厘米　厚 0.2~0.45 厘米

青绿玉质，温润柔和，透亮莹润。用钻孔和砣具镂空透雕
出相背而立的两只兽，呈昂首张口状，沁色过度自然，雕
琢细致，下端两边各有一钻孔，作为穿系佩戴用。

226 兽面形玉佩

长 5.95 厘米　宽 3.5 厘米　厚 0.21 厘米

青黄玉质，温润柔和。两只大圆眼，边缘成锯齿状，局部受沁呈
黄褐色，顶端有一穿，作为穿系佩戴用，近似于红山文化玉勾云
形佩。

227 蛇形玉佩

长 7.24 厘米　宽 0.65~1.15 厘米　厚 0.25~0.38 厘米

黄玉质，温润细腻，莹润透亮。身体部位雕琢自然，
蜿蜒爬行状，昂首张口，沁色柔和，过渡自然。

228 鸟形玉佩

长 7.6 厘米　宽 3 厘米　厚 0.25~0.3 厘米

青白玉质，温润细腻。系片状玉，通身素面无纹，
局部裂绺处受沁呈深褐色和灰白色，形似一鸟，
长尾上卷，尖喙。

229 鱼形玉佩

长 10.65 厘米　宽 1.5~2.4 厘米　厚 0.28 厘米

白玉质，莹润细腻，透亮有光泽。素面无纹，局部受沁呈
黄褐色和灰白色。鱼身，口部一穿。背部用扉棱勾勒出背
鳍，尾为双叉形，略向外撇。

230 鹰形玉佩（一对）

（上）长 9.3 厘米　宽 3.6 厘米　厚 0.1~0.28 厘米

（下）长 7.1 厘米　宽 3.6 厘米　厚 0.1~0.28 厘米

青绿玉质，细腻温润。局部受沁呈灰白色和黑色斑点，通体素面无纹。翅翼微翘，或上卷，头部和尾部各有一单面钻孔，其中一个有残缺。

231 动物形玉佩

长 6.68 厘米　宽 2.03 厘米　厚 0.4~0.5 厘米

青白玉质，莹润细腻，透亮纯净。通身素面无纹，局
部受沁呈黄褐色。头部和尾部雕琢成凸棱，为璇玑改
制而成。

232 鱼形玉佩

长 11.84 厘米　宽 3.28~5.55 厘米　厚 0.45 厘米

青白玉质，褐色条纹状纹理，莹润细腻。素面无纹，局
部受沁呈黄褐色条纹状。眼部有一横穿，背部和腹部为
锯齿状鳍。

234 动物形玉佩

长 6.1 厘米　宽 3.4 厘米　厚 0.3 厘米

青白玉质，温润细腻。体片状，局部受沁呈灰白色。整体
呈伏卧状，头部近三角形，嘴微张，尾部上翘。应为璇玑
残片改制，口部有一横穿。

235 动物形玉佩

长 5.9 厘米　宽 4 厘米　厚 0.7 厘米

绿松石质。体片状，局部受沁呈褐色和黑色。单面钻孔为眼，
口部呈凹坑状，留有管钻痕迹。尾部有一单面钻孔。整体制作
不甚规整，有人工切割痕迹。

236 鸟形玉佩

长 6 厘米　宽 2.8 厘米　厚 0.4 厘米

青黄玉质，温润细腻。体片状，局部受沁呈灰白色。鸟形，尖喙，眼部为一单面钻孔，颈部略束，足部有一横穿。

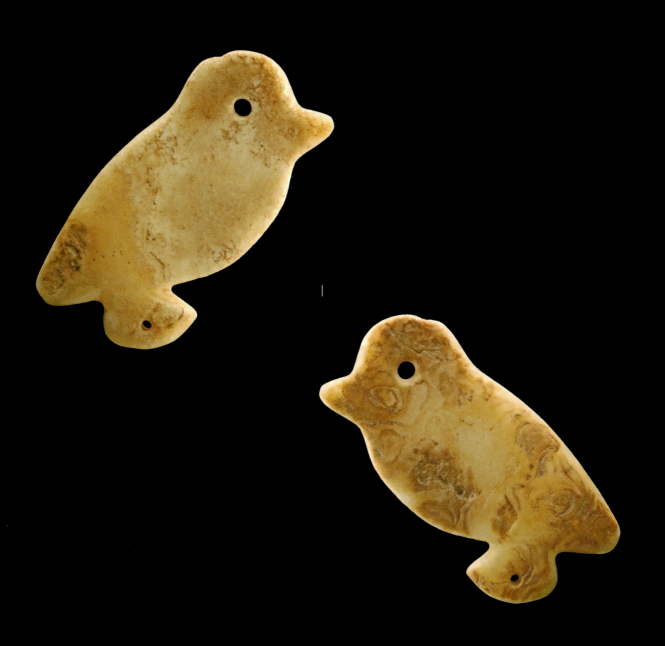

237 动物形玉佩

长 4.2 厘米　宽 3.8 厘米　厚 0.3 厘米

白玉质，温润细腻，透亮有光泽。体片状，局部受沁呈褐色。呈
蹲卧状，侧视，长耳后伏，嘴微张。头部有一横穿。

一

238 玉 觿

长9厘米　宽3.5厘米　厚0.5厘米

青黄玉质，温润细腻。沁色柔和，过渡自然，呈弧形，一端平
直，一端呈尖状。整体器型呈侧面人像。

239 鸟形玉佩（一对）

右 长 2.85 厘米　宽 1.81~1.86 厘米　厚 0.0.2 厘米

左 长 2.81 厘米　宽 1.0~1.85 厘米　厚 0.23 厘米

青黄玉质，温润细腻。体片状，为一对，局部受沁呈褐色。勾喙，
眼部由一钻孔琢出，颈部略束，弧形向下双翅外倾。

240 鸟形玉佩

长 5.9 厘米　宽 2.8 厘米

青白玉质,温润细腻。体片状,局部受沁呈灰白色及褐色。

鸟作蹲伏状,勾喙,嘴微张,足部有一横穿。

241 鸟形玉佩

长 6.2 厘米　宽 2.9 厘米

青白玉质，温润细腻。体片状，局部受沁呈灰白色和褐色，嘴微张，昂
头，颈部略束，背部雕琢出扉棱，尾部略上翘，下部有一横穿。

242 动物形玉佩

长 4.1 厘米　宽 2.4 厘米

青白玉质，温润细腻，透亮有光泽。体片状，局部受沁呈褐色和灰白色。头部有两个单面钻孔，其中一孔旁有管钻痕迹。

243 蝉形玉佩

长 3.8 厘米　宽 3.3 厘米

青玉质，受沁严重。局部受沁呈褐色和灰白色。头部有
个单面钻孔，表面有阴刻弦纹。

黄玉质，青白玉质。坠为环形饰，串饰为不规则的圆珠状，打磨光滑。

十六 串 饰

244 玉串饰

玉坠长 5.35 厘米　宽 3.9 厘米　厚 8.5 厘米

大孔径 1.3~1.55 厘米　外径 2.5~2.9 厘米

小孔径 0.48 厘米　外径 0.7 厘米

黄玉质，青白玉质。坠为环形饰，串饰为不规则的圆珠状，打磨光滑。

245 绿松石串饰

长 39 厘米
小玉璧　直径 2.9 厘米
孔径 0.8 厘米　厚 0.4 厘米
玉珠为绿松石质，形状不规则，打磨
较为光滑，下端配有白玉璧，玉质温
润，有沁色。

246 白玉串饰

玉坠长 2.1 厘米

串饰为白玉珠磨制而成，下端配有一三角形人面坠和绿松
石管珠，单行穿成。

247 玉组佩（一套）

玉环直径（大）5.2 厘米

由三件环、五件小玉璜组成，璜两端皆
有穿孔，大璜有断裂，后修复。

248 玉串饰

玉管均长 1.2~3.5 厘米

由绿松石、白玉、叶蜡石组成，打磨光滑，形状不规则，其中
玉管有人工切割的痕迹。

249 绿松石串饰

绿松石管均长 2.2~3.7 厘米

由 9 颗绿松石组成，打磨光滑，形状不规则。

250 绿松石串饰

绿松石珠均长 1.4~2.3 厘米

由绿松石组成，打磨光滑，形状不规则，共有 17 颗。

十七 玉 簪

—

251 玉 簪

长 23 厘米　宽 1.2 厘米　厚 0.47 厘米

白玉质，莹润透亮。扁长体，一端出榫头，另一端收锋呈尖状，打磨光滑，通
体素面无纹，局部受沁呈褐色和灰白色，沁色柔和，过渡自然。

252 玉 簪

长 17.2 厘米　宽 1.29 厘米　厚 0.67 厘米

白玉质，莹润细腻，透亮有光泽。扁长体，一端收锋
呈尖状，一端有一单面钻孔，打磨光滑，通体光素无
纹，局部受沁呈灰白色。

十八　玉刻刀

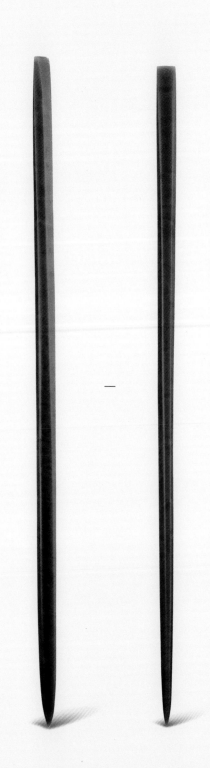

253 玉刻刀

长 23 厘米　宽 0.65~0.73 厘米　厚 0.73 厘米

青黄玉质，莹润透亮，温润细腻。呈多棱体形，一端为尖
锥状，一端为扁平口，局部受沁呈灰白色。

254 玉刻刀

长 12.6 厘米　宽 1.35 厘米　厚 0.5 厘米

白玉质，温润透亮。略呈尖首长条状，通体素面无纹，表面受
沁呈灰白色，一端平直，有一单面钻孔。

255 玉刻刀

长 19.3 厘米　宽 1.43 厘米　厚 0.63 厘米

青绿玉质，细腻温润。呈扁平长方体形，一端为尖刃状，
磨制锋利尖锐，一端呈弧形，局部受沁呈灰白色。

256 玉刻刀

长 15 厘米　宽 1.8 厘米　厚 0.6 厘米

白玉质，温润细腻，透亮有光泽。呈尖首长条状，上
下宽度雷同，素面无纹，表面受沁呈黄褐色和灰白色。
两面中部起脊，另一端呈刃状，有一单面钻孔痕迹。

十九　玉锥形器

257 玉锥形器

长 9.94 厘米　直径 1.1~1.19 厘米

白玉质，细腻温润，有光泽。呈圆柱体，为石家河文化的鹰形玉笄首改制而成，隐约可见隐起的羽翅，两端磨成刃状，其中一端有残缺，近中部有一单面钻。

青白玉质，细腻温润，有光泽。用石家河文化的
玉簪首改制而成，中部横穿一孔，单面钻成，两
端磨成钻头状，有人工切割痕迹。

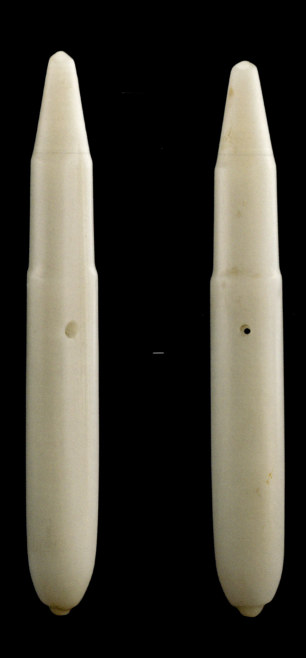

左 长 6.62 厘米　直径 1.15 厘米
中 长 8.5 厘米　直径 0.48~0.95 厘米
右 长 7.1 厘米　直径 1 厘米
白玉质，细腻温润。呈圆锥状，局部受沁呈红褐色和灰
白色。用石家河文化的玉簪首改制而成，一端加工成钻
头形，其中一个腰身有一横穿，一个腰身有两横穿，均
为单面钻孔。

260 玉锥形器（一组三件）

左 长 3.89 厘米　直径 0.65 厘米
中 长 4.5 厘米　直径 1.18~1.32 厘米
右 长 4.49 厘米　直径 0.5~0.7 厘米

青绿彩石质，有云母状结晶杂质。呈圆锥状，
局部绺裂处受沁呈黄褐色，其中一个为麻
花钻。

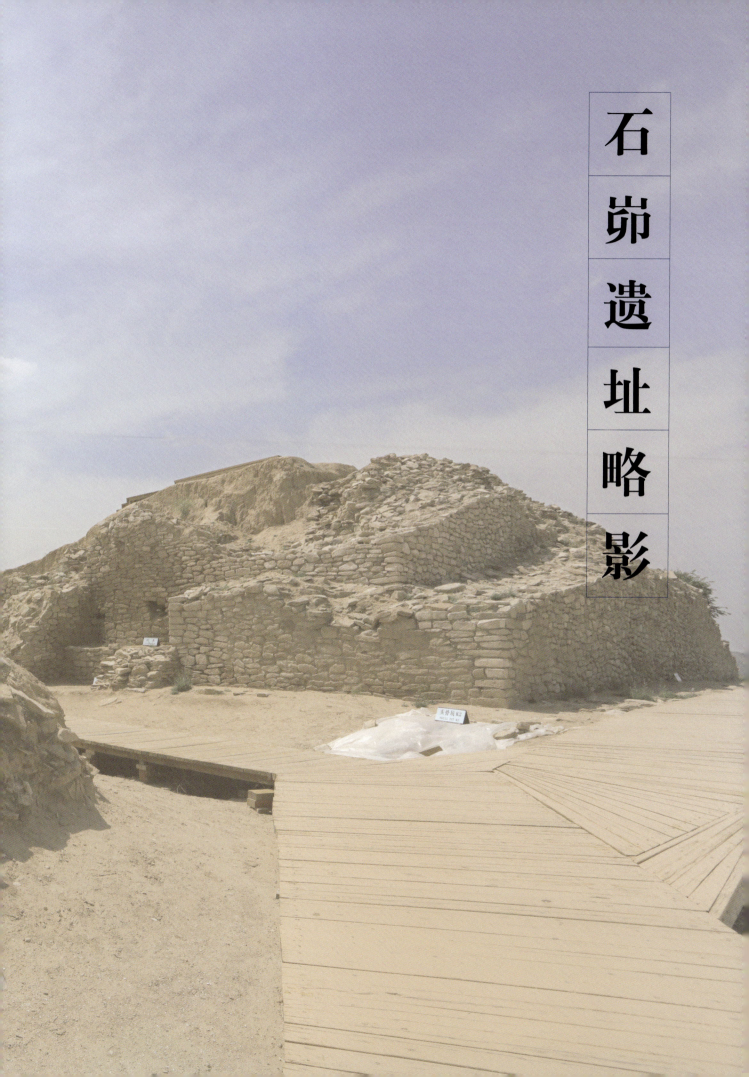

石峁遗址略影

石峁古城遗址东门全景

石峁古城遗址东门门道

石峁古城遗址东门墙体

石峁古城遗址东门石砌墙体状况

门塾内结构

皇城台遗址全景

皇城台遗址前广场石砌墙基

皇城台遗址石砌护坡

皇城台遗址顶部宫殿区池苑遗址

后 记

千年古玉遭流失　　牵动华夏儿女心
坚持追索数十载　　辑精付梓补初心

　　拙作《石峁玉器》即将与同仁们见面了，回想那不平凡的追索、编撰之路，感慨万千，一言难尽。欣慰的是多年来，我们在各级政府部门的大力支持下，曾经的梦想终于变成了现实。欣慰之余，诚挚地向一贯关心支持石峁文化研究的陕西省文物局、陕西省考古研究院、北京大学震旦古代文明研究中心、美国斯坦福大学、榆林市文广新局、神木市市委、神木市人民政府、石峁遗址管理处、神木市文体广电局、民政局、神木市博物馆以及中国文化艺术发展促进会收藏文化专业委员会、陕西省收藏家协会等单位，向具体指导和关心我们的北京大学教授李伯谦、上海交通大学教授叶舒宪、中国文化艺术发展促进会收藏文化专业委员会主任古方、秘书长向东，文物出版社编辑徐旸、摄影师宋朝，《收藏家》杂志编辑李红娟、陕西省林业厅厅长李三原、陕西省文物局原副局长刘云辉、陕西省考古研究院院长孙周勇、陕西省历史博物馆副书记兼副馆长王炜林、陕西省文物保护研究院副院长王保平、台湾杨建芳师生古玉研究会会长陈启贤、河南省驻马店市博物馆张勇、石峁遗址考古队队长邵晶、榆林市文研所原所长康兰英、原神木县文广局局长现任榆林技术学院神木校区党委副书记项世荣、神木市文体广电局局长李建军、神木镇党委书记苏永华等专家、同仁，表示衷心的感谢，并致以崇高的敬意！特别感谢神木市书协主席孙世瑾同志为本书题写书名。

　　玉器是华夏民族起源的根脉，是人类文明进步的结晶，同时也是华夏历史上唯一没有间断过的珍贵文化崇拜现象。它不仅承载和积淀着不朽的玉文化精髓，同时也浸透着光辉灿烂的时代文明信息，是探寻中华文明起源、研究历史发展轨迹、总结人类文明进步过程中必不可少的实物史料。

　　石峁玉器是始于龙山文化晚期至夏代早期这段特殊历史时期的重要遗物，是研究论证石峁遗址遗存性质以及石峁文化发展的重要物证。由于各种客观因素，大批石峁玉器脱离了原始环境，流散于世界各地，这无疑对我们今天研究石峁遗址的历史文化和玉器史是一个巨大的缺陷。在这个关键时刻，石峁文化研究会主动承担起了"保护石峁遗址和抢救石峁文物"的重任，通过不懈的努力，不仅石峁遗址的发掘取得了"石破天惊"般的重大发现，而且石峁文物的抢救征集也硕果累累。今天我们以分享成果，提供资料的形式，首先选择有代表意义的石峁玉器编纂成书，展示给大家，希望本书的出版能起到一个拾遗补缺、推动研究的作用。

编　者

2017 年 10 月 8 日